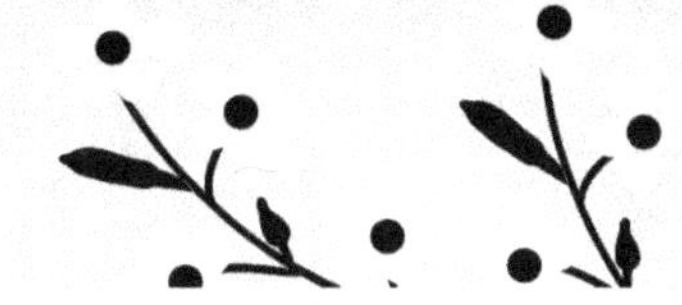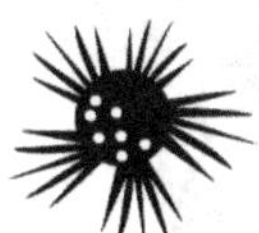

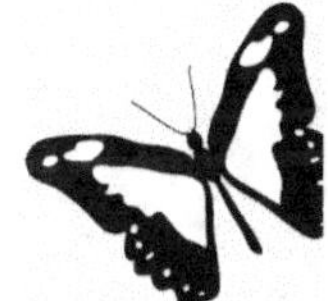

ISBN: 978-1-7354712-1-1

For information contact: Bharrisbooks.com

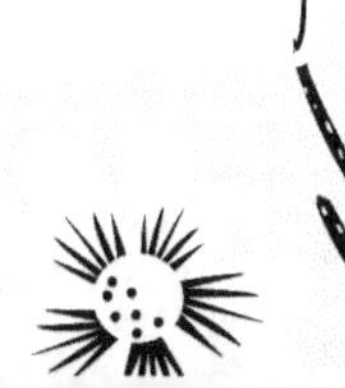

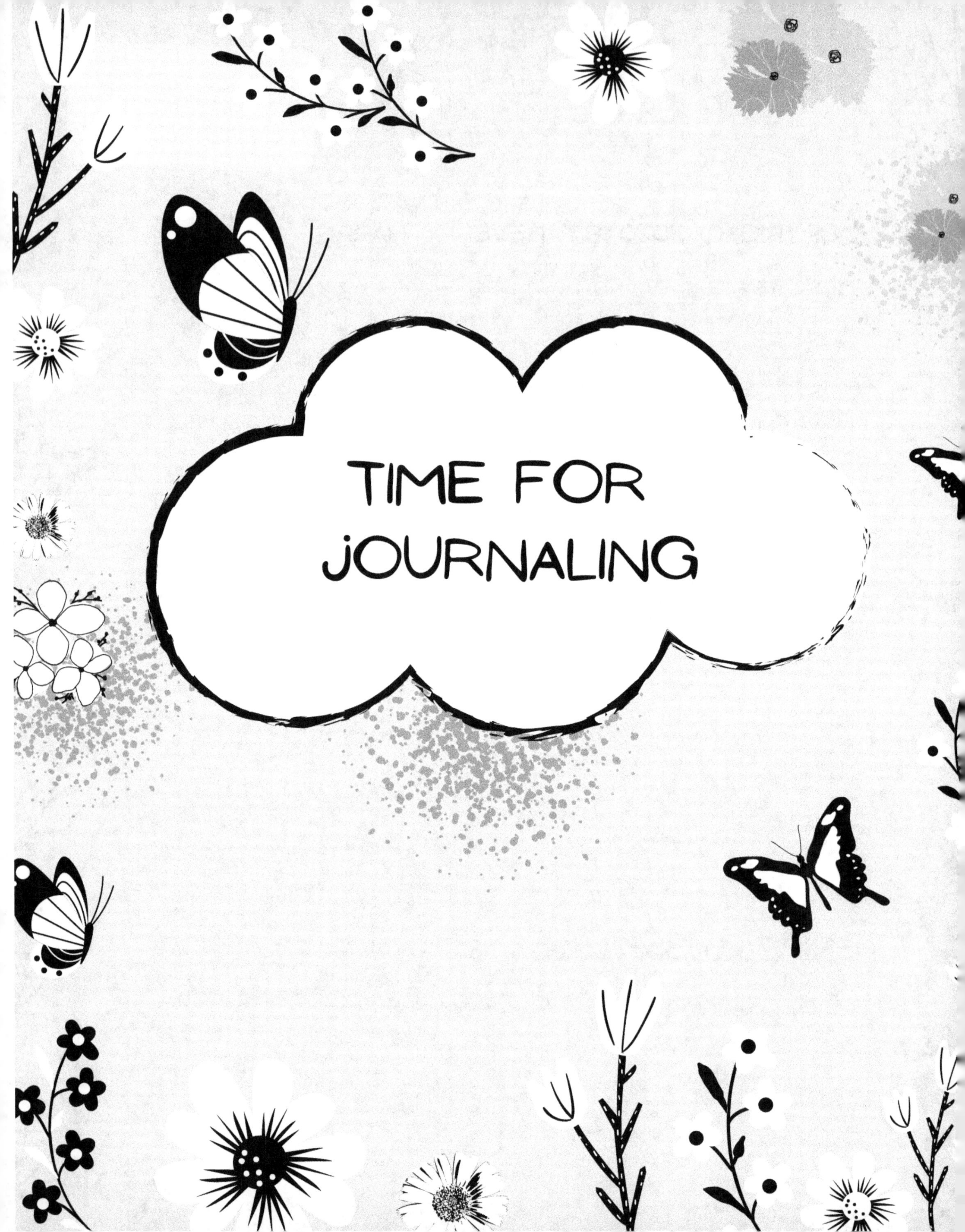
TIME FOR
JOURNALING

TIME FOR JOURNALING

MY SUPER POWER IS ME!

TIME FOR JOURNALING
DREAM

TIME FOR JOURNALING

YES!!

Joy!
Joy!
Joy!

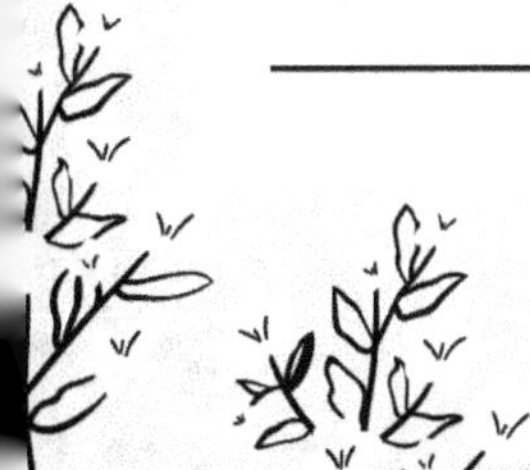

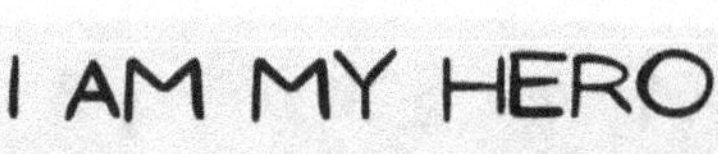
I AM MY HERO!

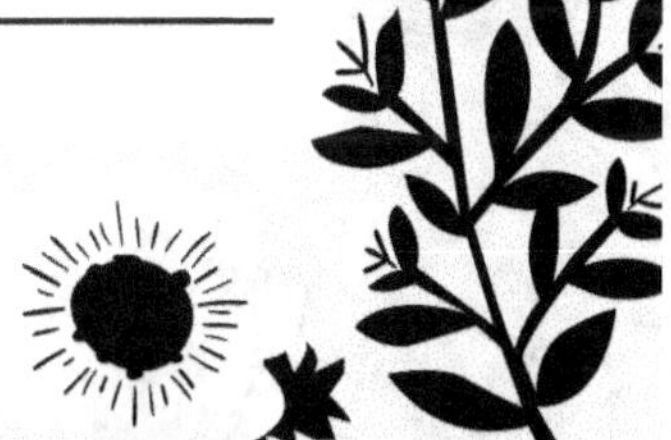

TIME FOR JOURNALING
WHAT'S UP?

TIME FOR JOURNALING

SOMETIMES CHANGE
CAN BE GOOD

TIME FOR JOURNALING

BREATHE

TIME FOR
JOURNALING

TODAY MY DAY WAS...

TIME FOR JOURNALING

GOOD THINGS HAPPEN
TO ME ALL OF THE TIME!

TIME FOR JOURNALING

____

____

____

____

____

____

____

____

____

____

____

SOAR

TIME FOR JOURNALING
I LOVE MYSELF AND OTHERS DO TOO!

MY SUPER POWER IS ME!

TIME FOR JOURNALING
DREAM

TIME FOR JOURNALING

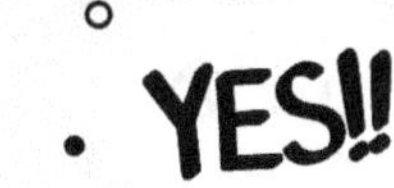

YES!!

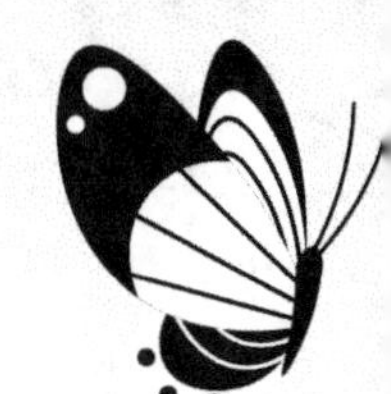

Joy!
Joy!
Joy!

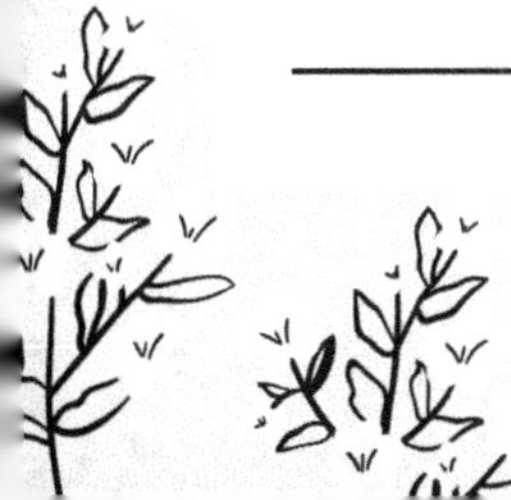

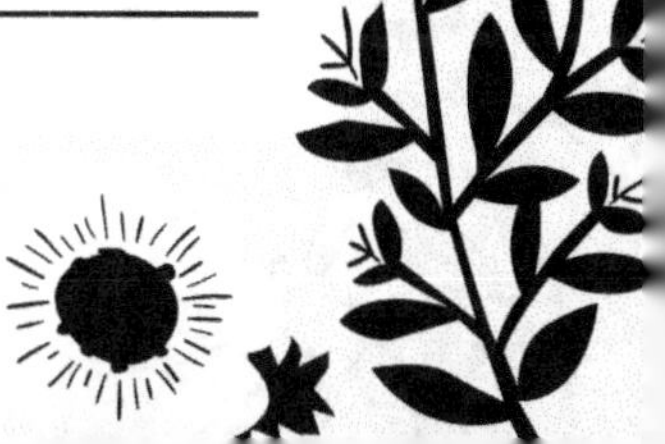

I AM MY HERO!

TIME FOR JOURNALING
WHAT'S UP?

TIME FOR JOURNALING

SOMETIMES CHANGE
CAN BE GOOD

TIME FOR JOURNALING
BREATHE

TIME FOR JOURNALING
TODAY MY DAY WAS...

TIME FOR
JOURNALING

GOOD THINGS HAPPEN
TO ME ALL OF THE TIME!

SOAR

I LOVE MYSELF AND
OTHERS DO TOO!

MY SUPER POWER IS ME!

DREAM

TIME FOR JOURNALING

YES!!

JOY!
JOY!
JOY!

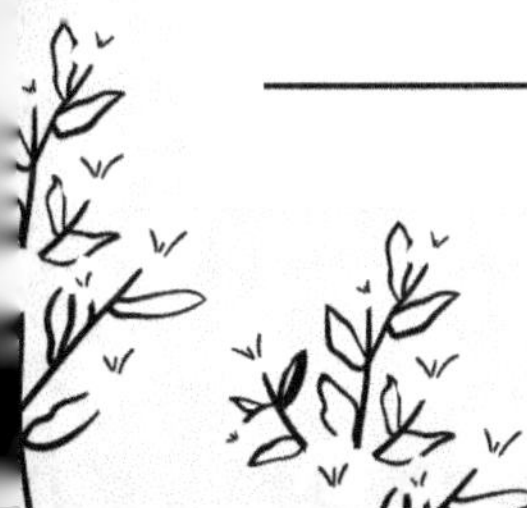

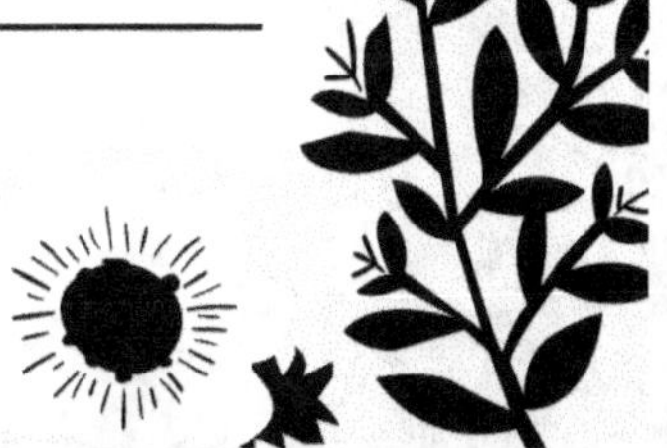

I AM MY HERO!

TIME FOR JOURNALING

WHAT'S UP?

TIME FOR JOURNALING

SOMETIMES CHANGE
CAN BE GOOD

TIME FOR JOURNALING

____
____
____
____
____
____
____
____
____
____
____
____
____

BREATHE

TIME FOR JOURNALING

TODAY MY DAY WAS...

TIME FOR JOURNALING

GOOD THINGS HAPPEN
TO ME ALL OF THE TIME!

SOAR

TIME FOR JOURNALING
I LOVE MYSELF AND OTHERS DO TOO!

MY SUPER POWER IS ME!

TIME FOR JOURNALING

DREAM

TIME FOR JOURNALING

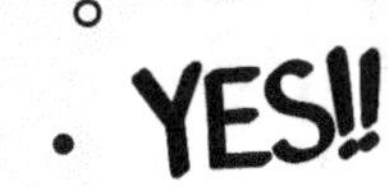

YES!!

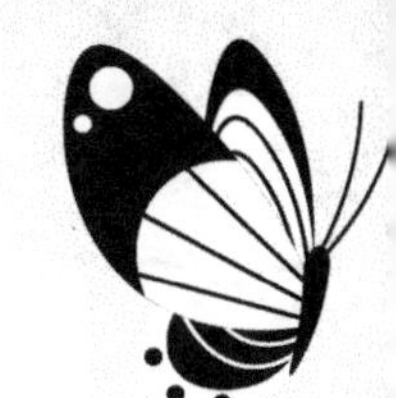

Joy!
Joy!
Joy!

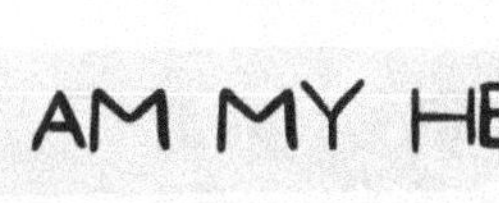

I AM MY HERO!

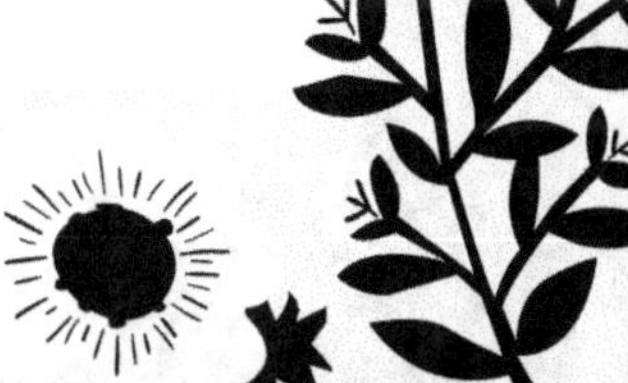

TIME FOR JOURNALING
WHAT'S UP?

TIME FOR
JOURNALING

SOMETIMES CHANGE
CAN BE GOOD

TIME FOR JOURNALING
BREATHE

TIME FOR JOURNALING
TODAY MY DAY WAS...

GOOD THINGS HAPPEN
TO ME ALL OF THE TIME!

SOAR

TIME FOR JOURNALING

I LOVE MYSELF AND
OTHERS DO TOO!

TIME FOR
JOURNALING

MY SUPER POWER IS ME!

TIME FOR JOURNALING
DREAM

TIME FOR
JOURNALING

YES!!

JOY!
JOY!
JOY!

I AM MY HERO!

TIME FOR JOURNALING
WHAT'S UP?

TIME FOR JOURNALING

SOMETIMES CHANGE
CAN BE GOOD

TIME FOR JOURNALING
BREATHE

TIME FOR JOURNALING
TODAY MY DAY WAS...

TIME FOR JOURNALING

GOOD THINGS HAPPEN
TO ME ALL OF THE TIME!

TIME FOR JOURNALING

SOAR

TIME FOR JOURNALING

I LOVE MYSELF AND
OTHERS DO TOO!

MY SUPER POWER IS ME!

TIME FOR JOURNALING
DREAM

TIME FOR JOURNALING

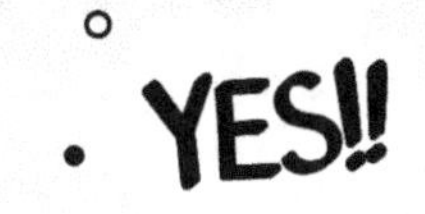
YES!!

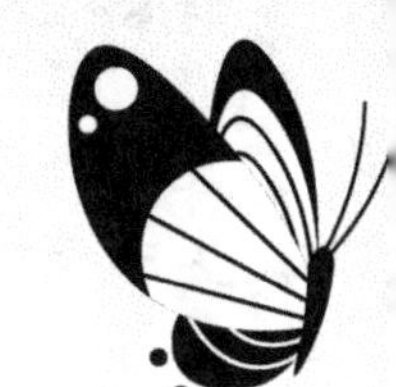

Joy!
Joy!
Joy!

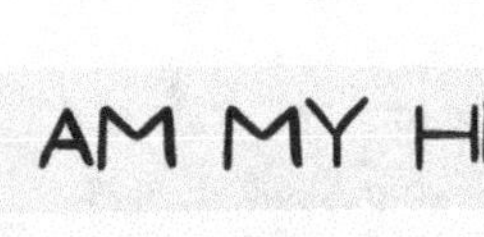
I AM MY HERO!

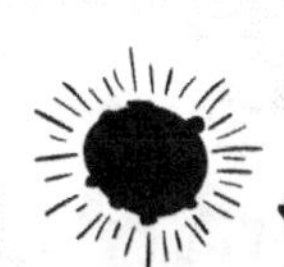

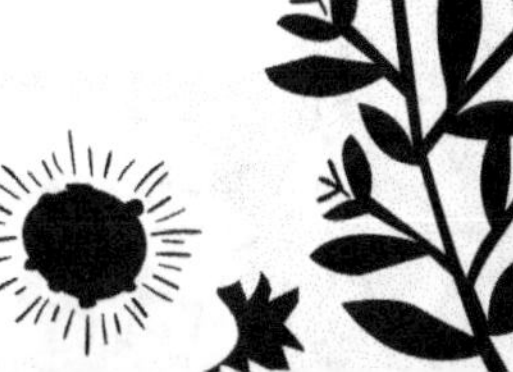

TIME FOR JOURNALING

WHAT'S UP?

SOMETIMES CHANGE
CAN BE GOOD

TIME FOR JOURNALING
BREATHE

TIME FOR JOURNALING

TODAY MY DAY WAS...

TIME FOR JOURNALING

GOOD THINGS HAPPEN
TO ME ALL OF THE TIME!

SOAR

TIME FOR
JOURNALING

I LOVE MYSELF AND
OTHERS DO TOO!

Time for
drawing

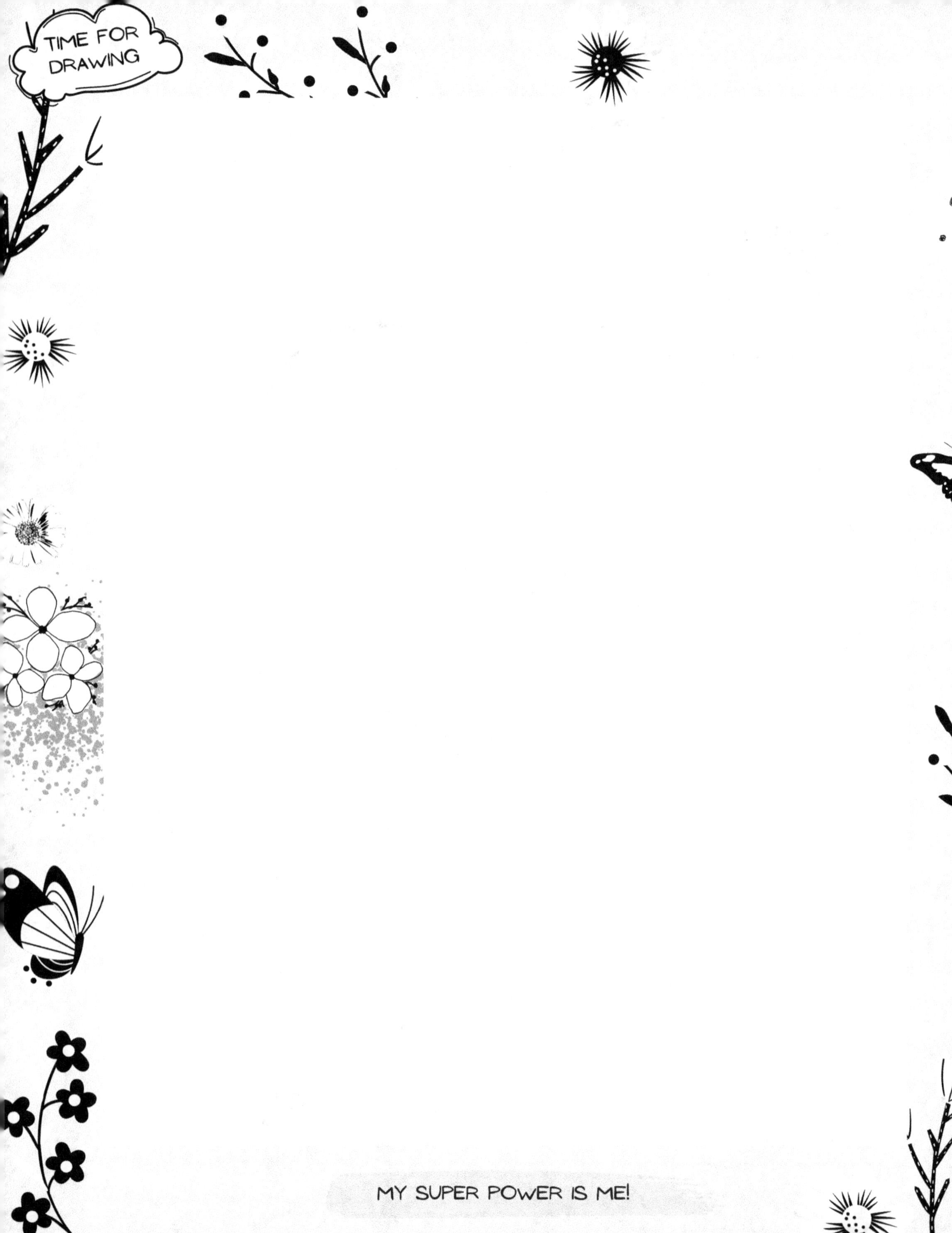

TIME FOR DRAWING
MY SUPER POWER IS ME!

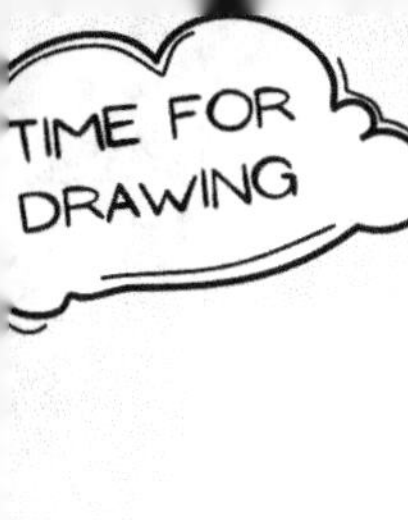

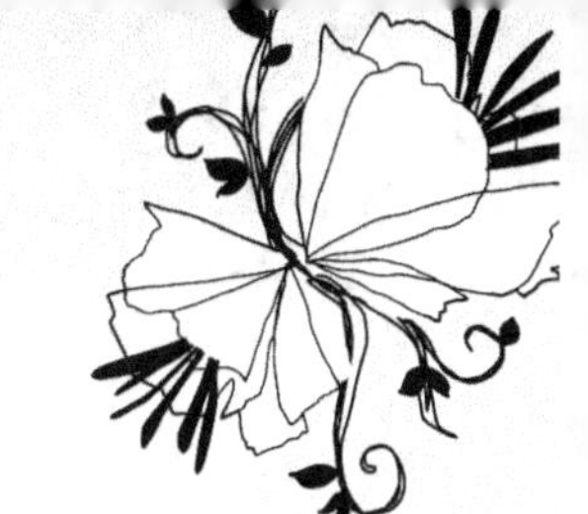

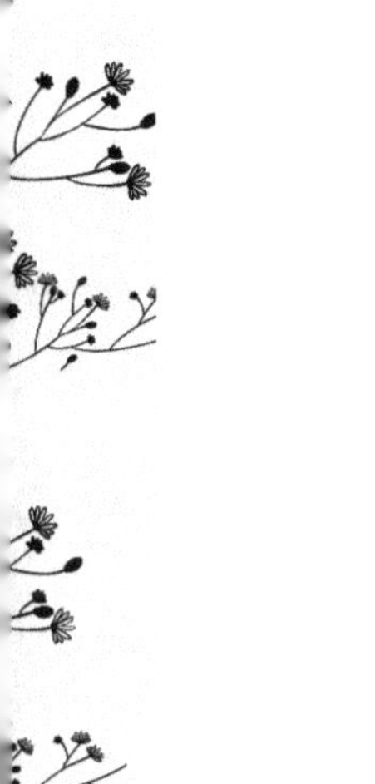

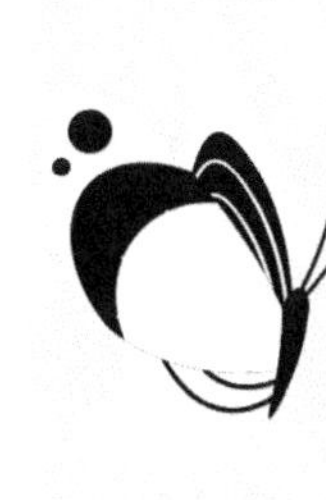

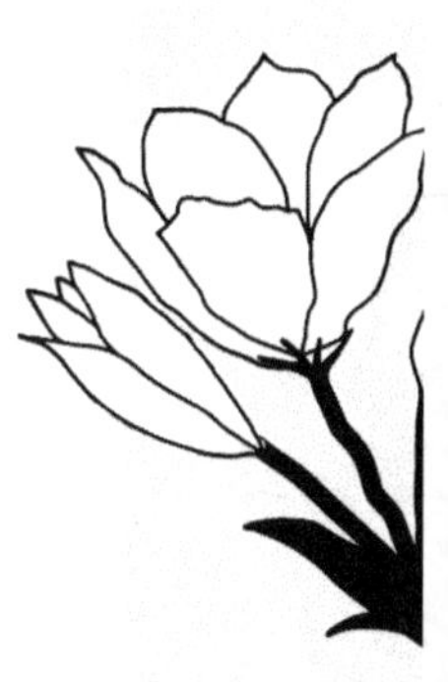

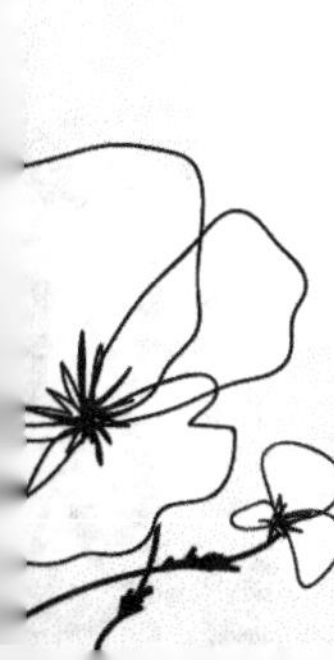

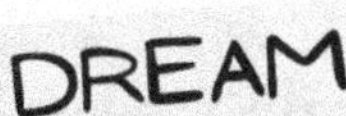

DREAM

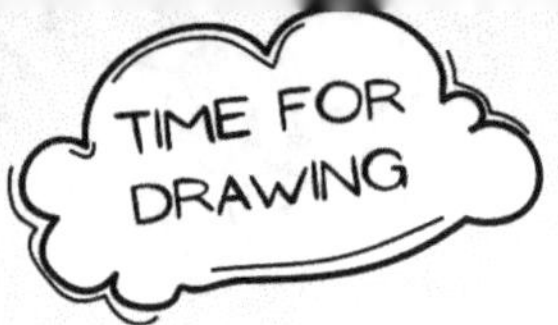

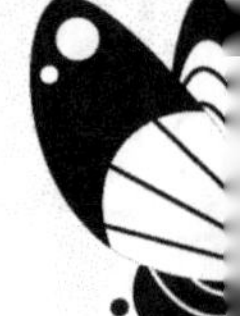

enjoy!
enjoy!
enjoy!

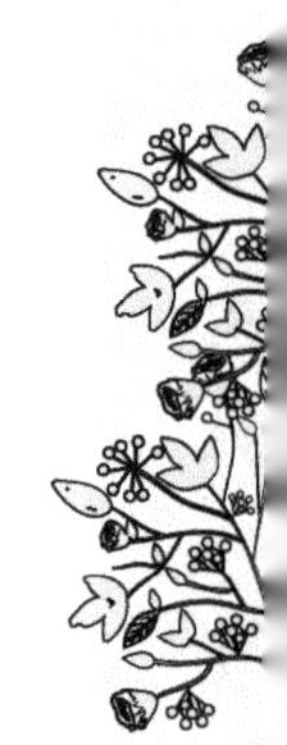

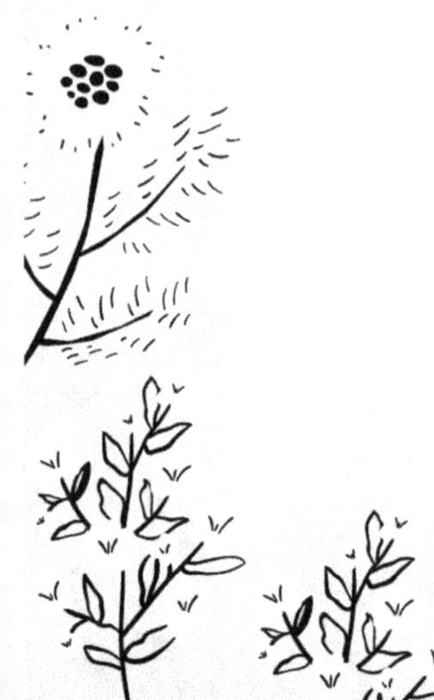

I AM MY HERO!

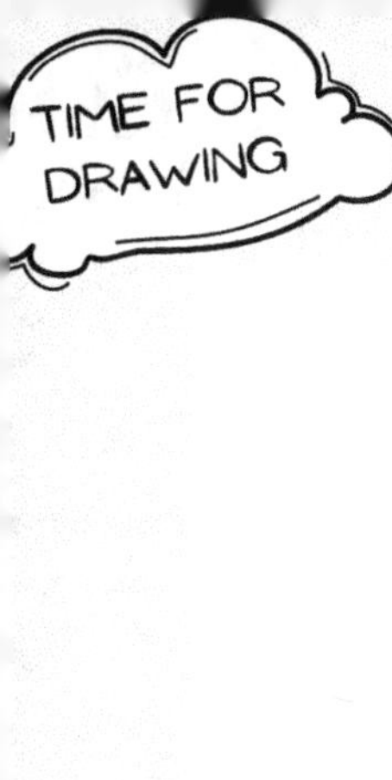
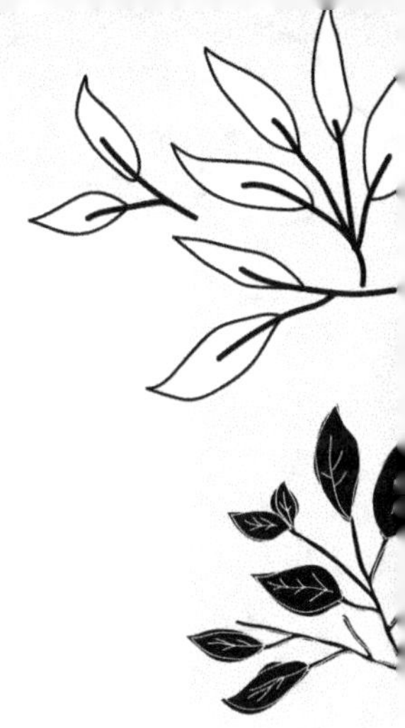

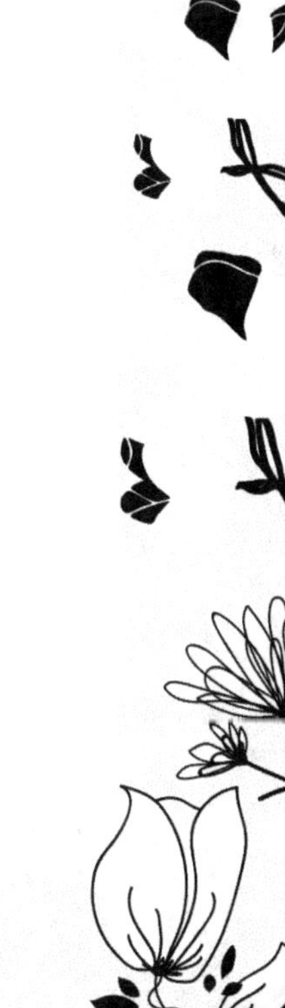

WHAT'S UP?

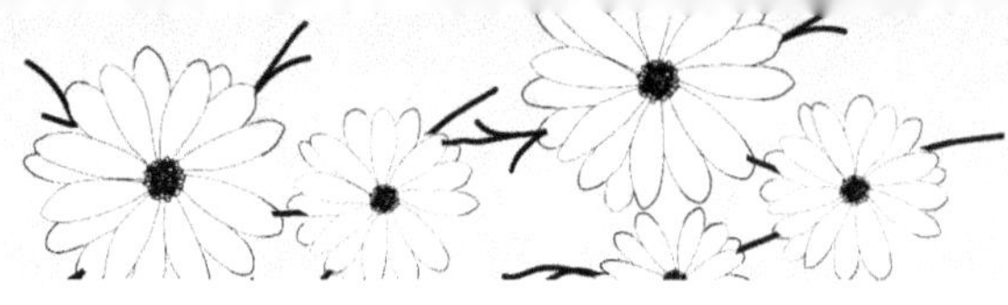

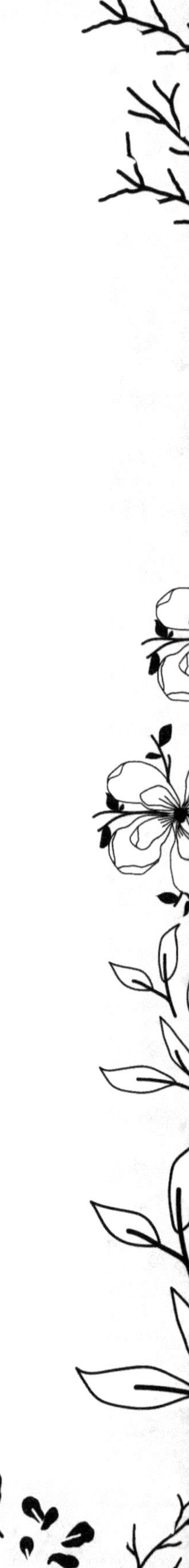
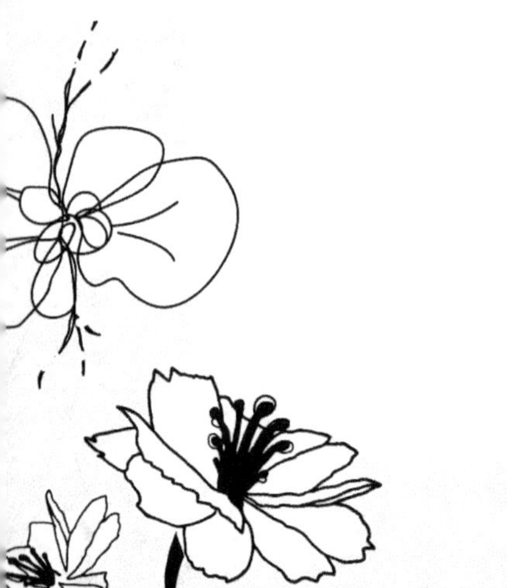

SOMETIMES CHANGE
CAN BE GOOD

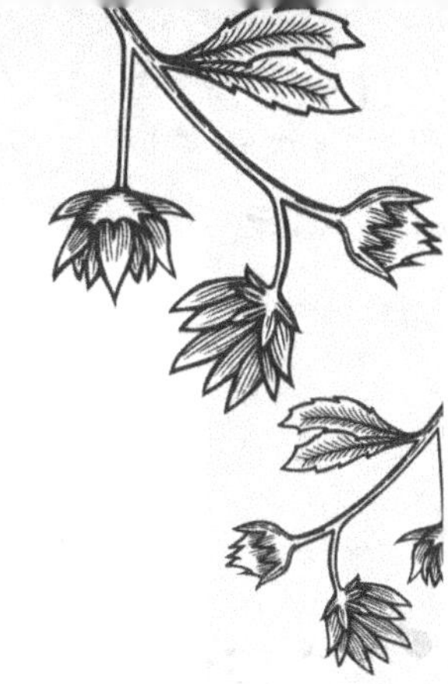

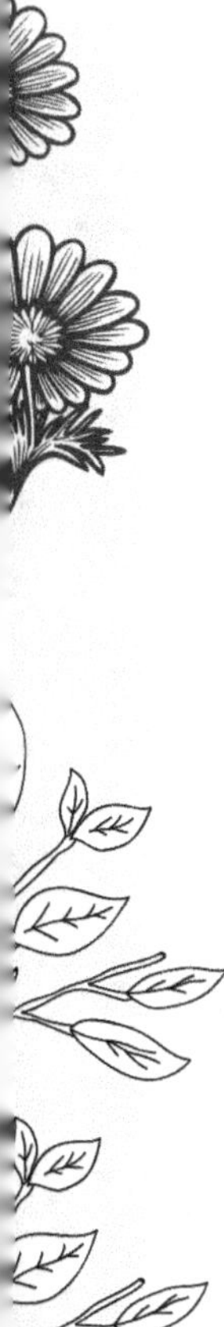

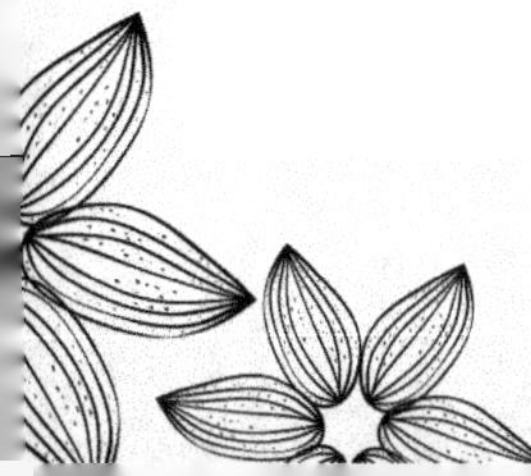

BREATHE

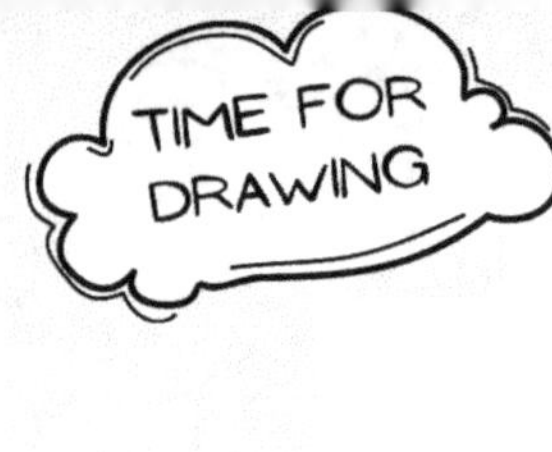

TIME FOR
DRAWING

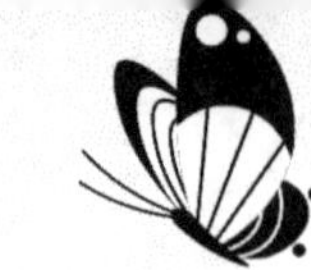

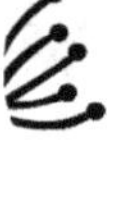

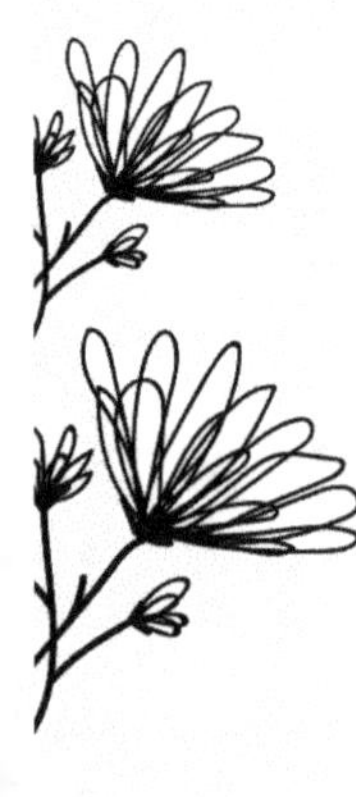
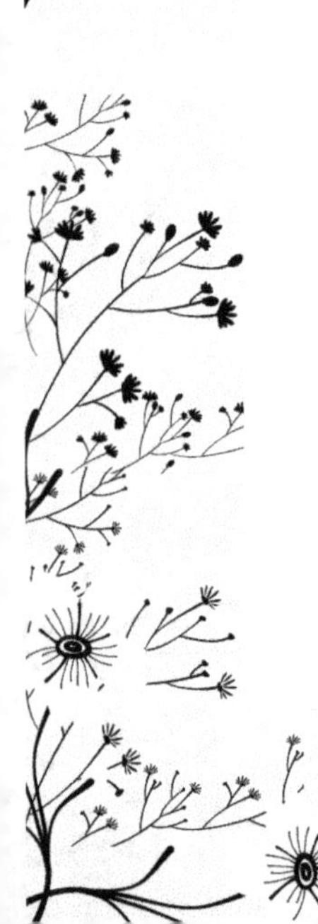
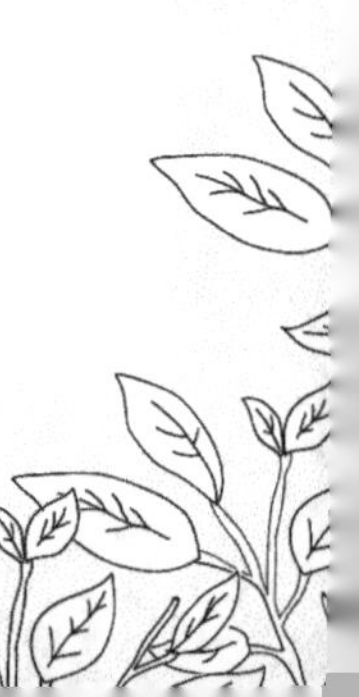

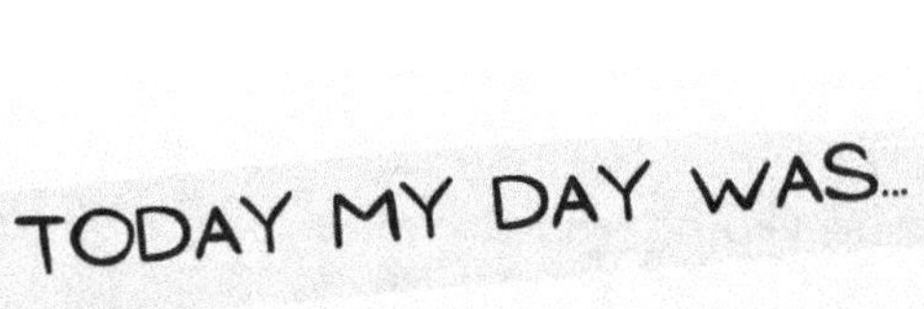

TODAY MY DAY WAS...

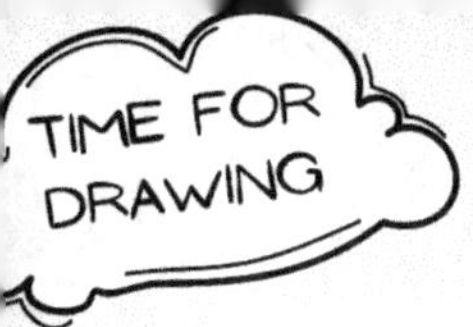

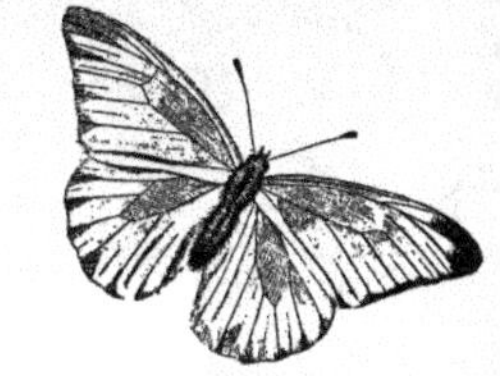

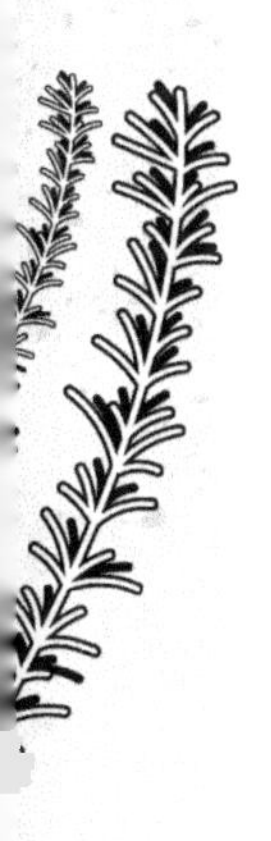

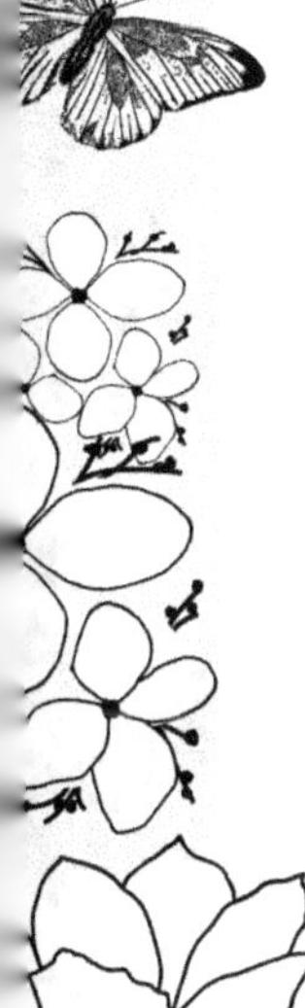

GOOD THINGS HAPPEN
TO ME ALL OF THE TIME!

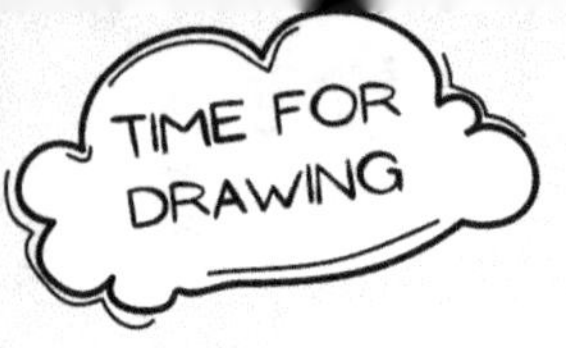

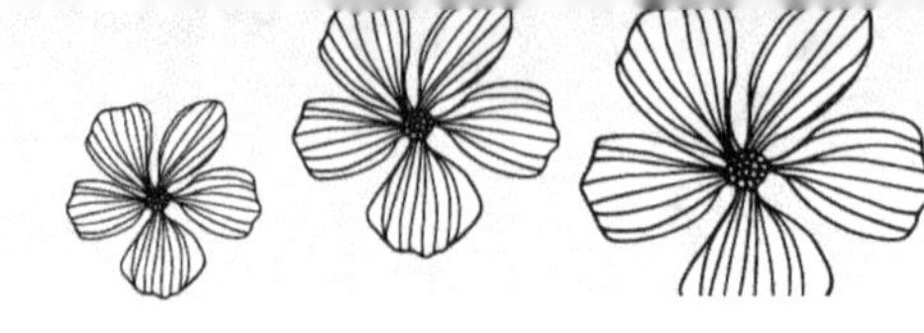

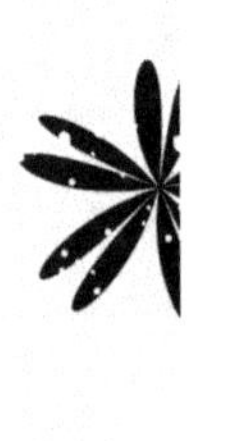

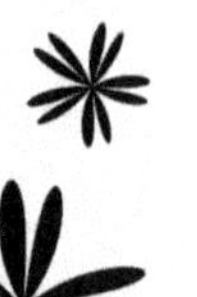

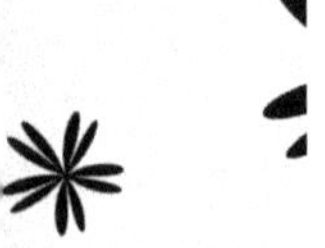

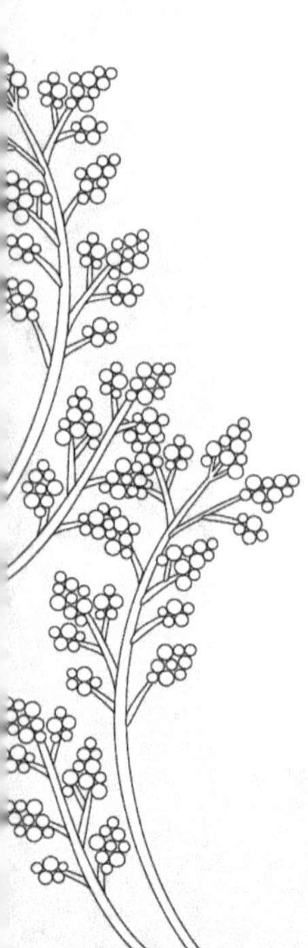

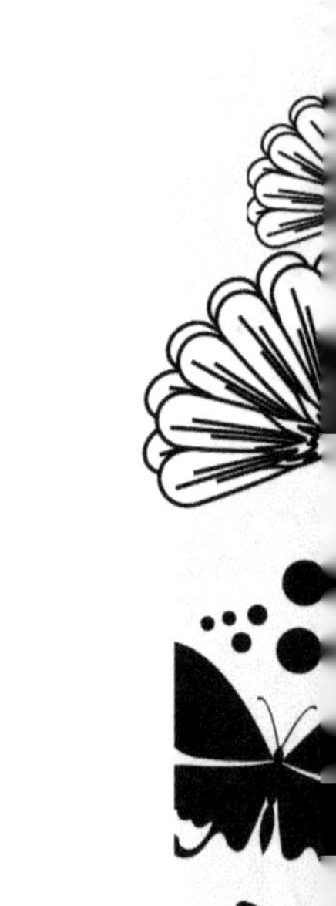

SOAR

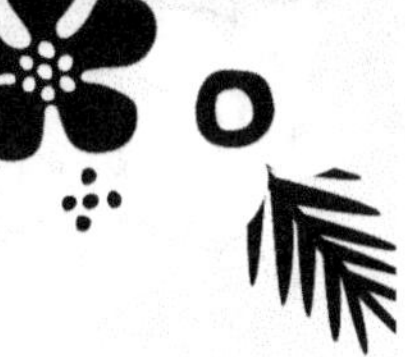

TIME FOR
DRAWING

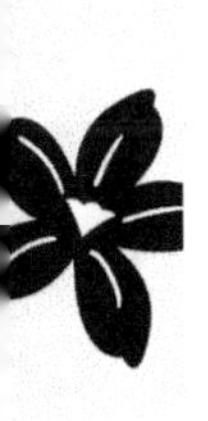

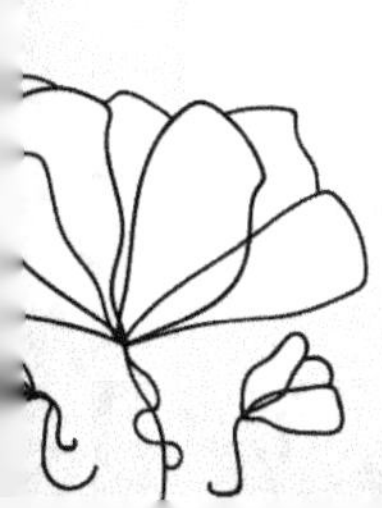

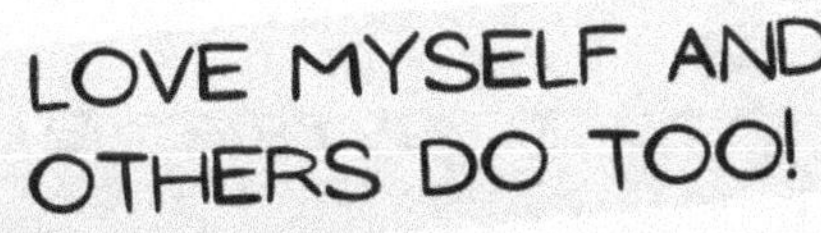

I LOVE MYSELF AND
OTHERS DO TOO!

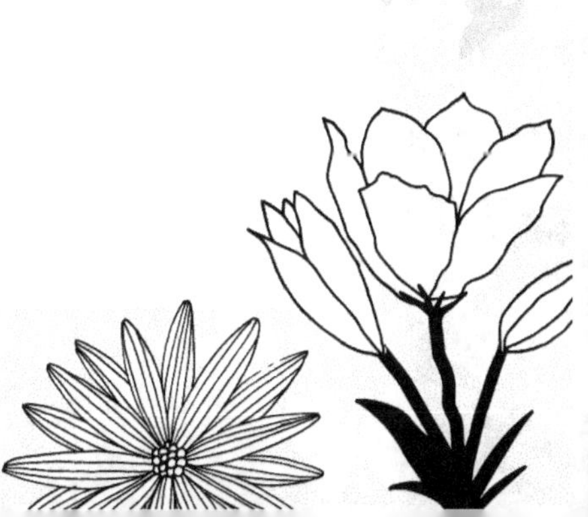

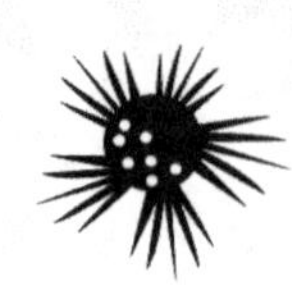
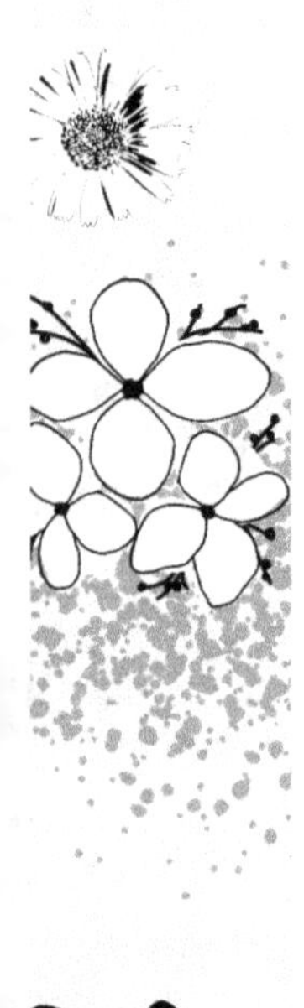
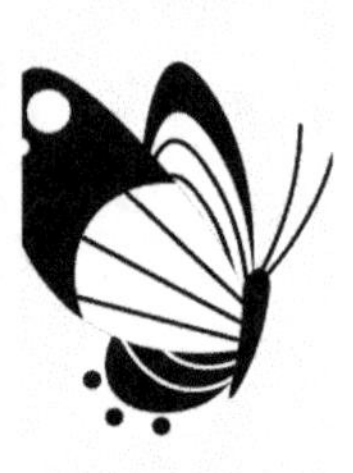
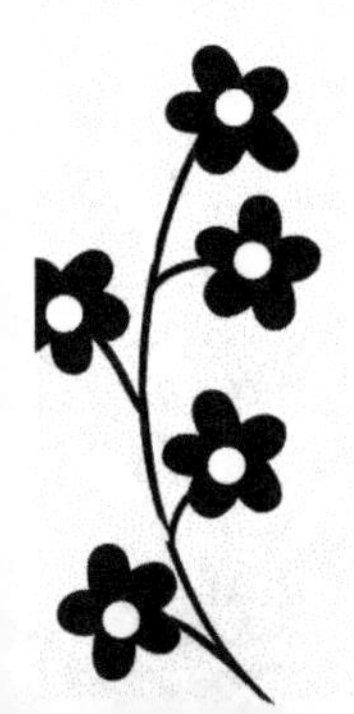
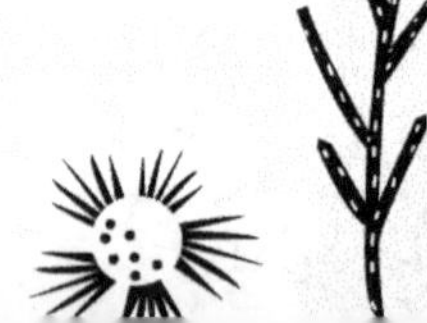

MY SUPER POWER IS ME!

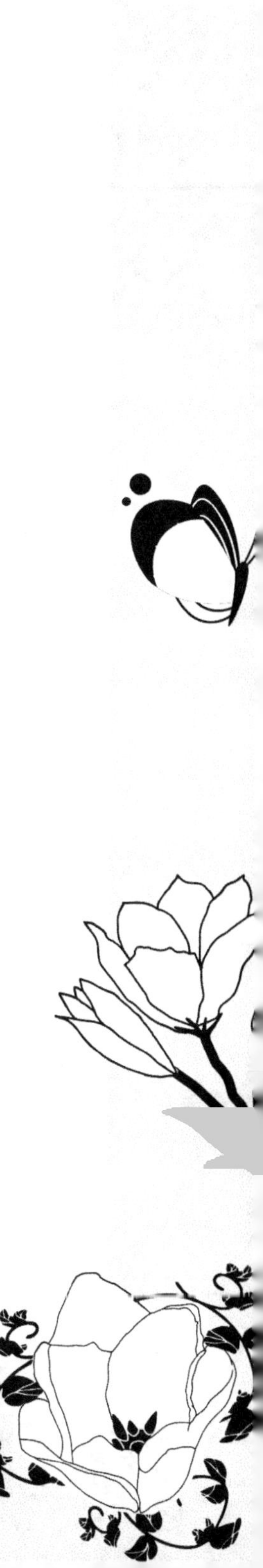

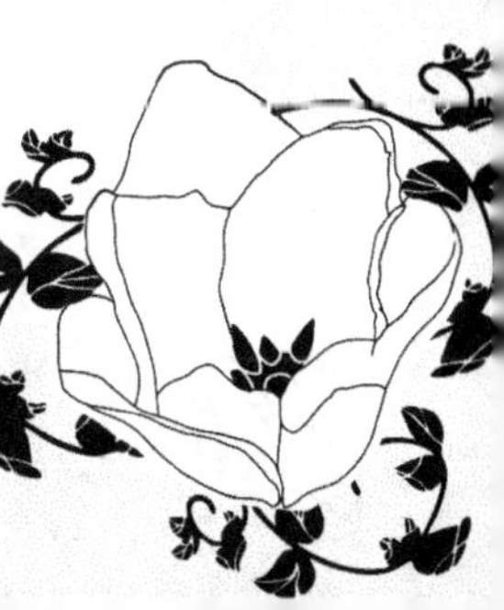

DREAM

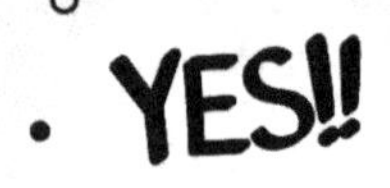

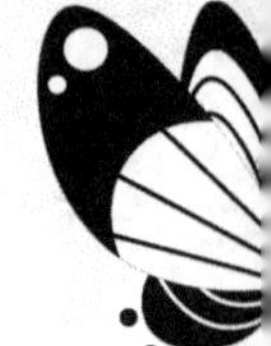

enjoy!
enjoy!
enjoy!

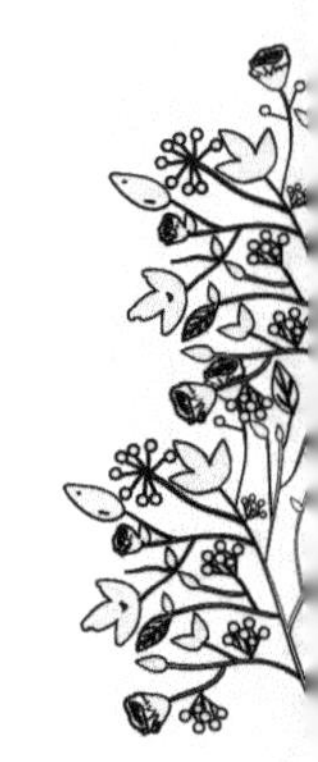

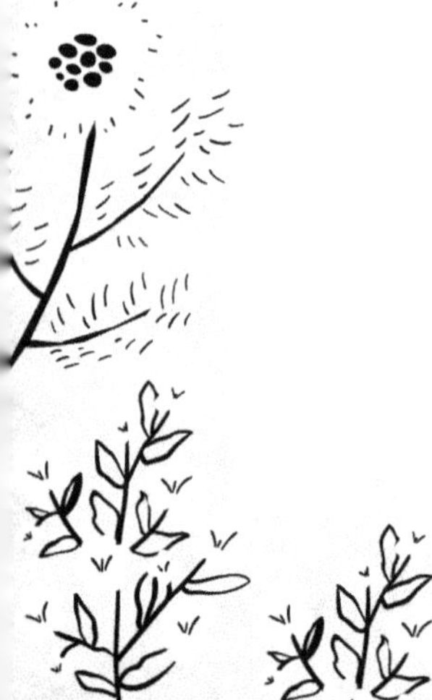

I AM MY HERO!

WHAT'S UP?

TIME FOR
DRAWING
SOMETIMES CHANGE
CAN BE GOOD

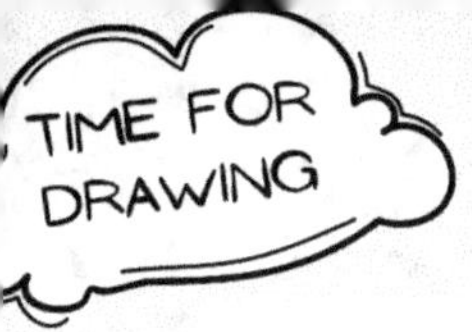

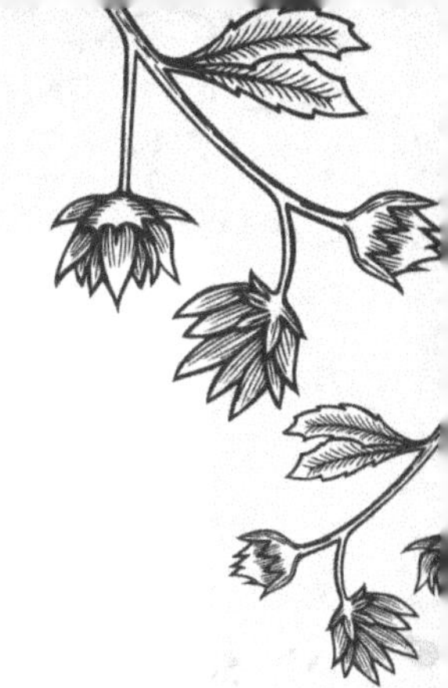

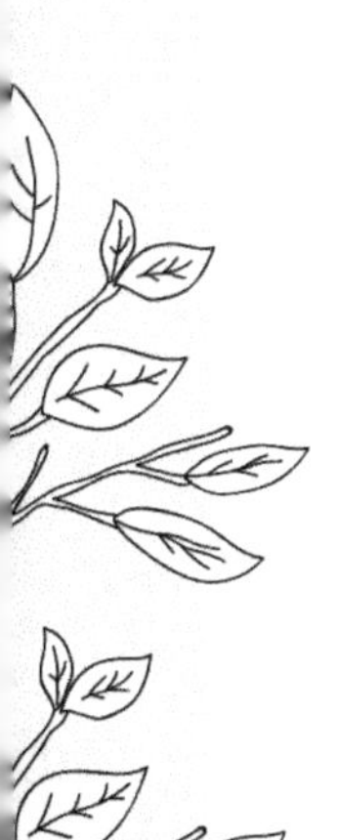

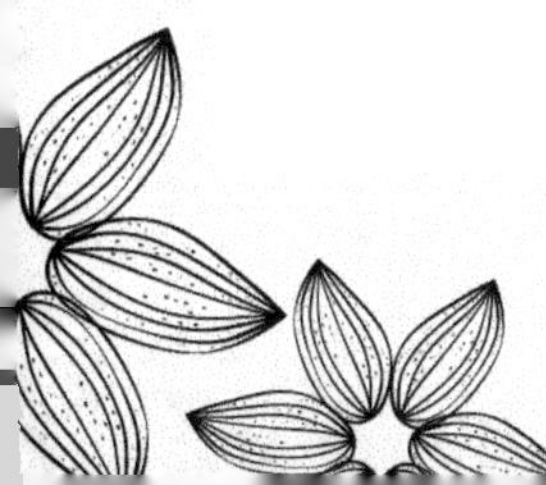

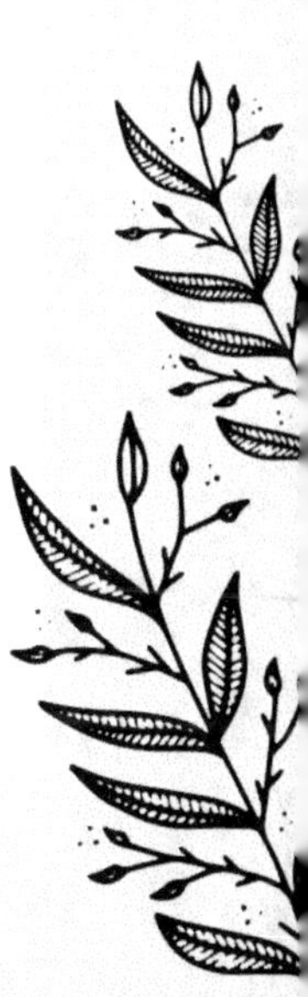

BREATHE

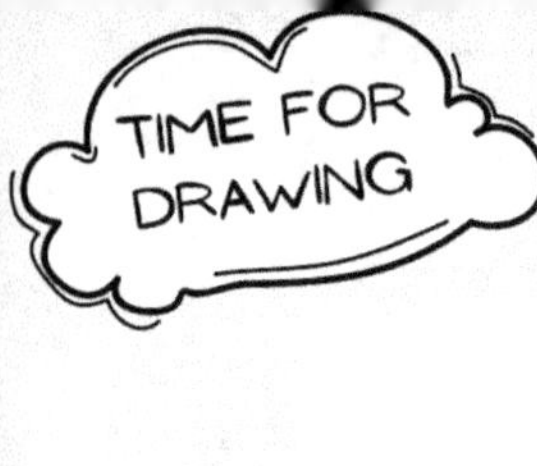

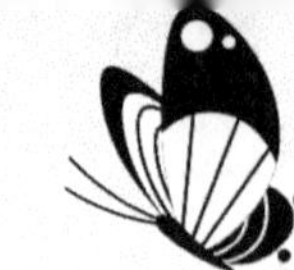

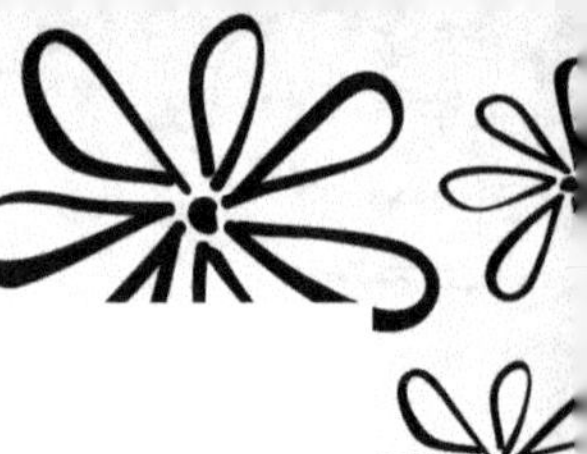

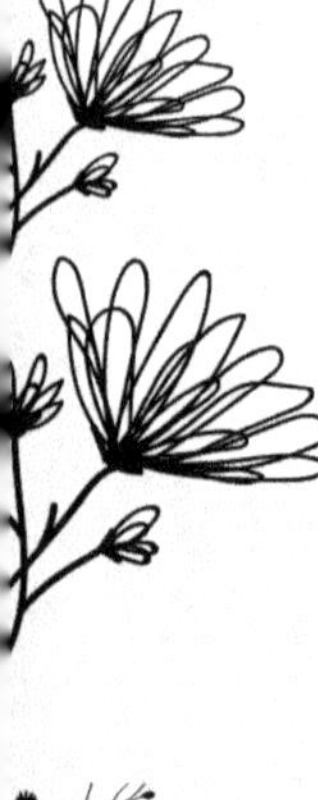

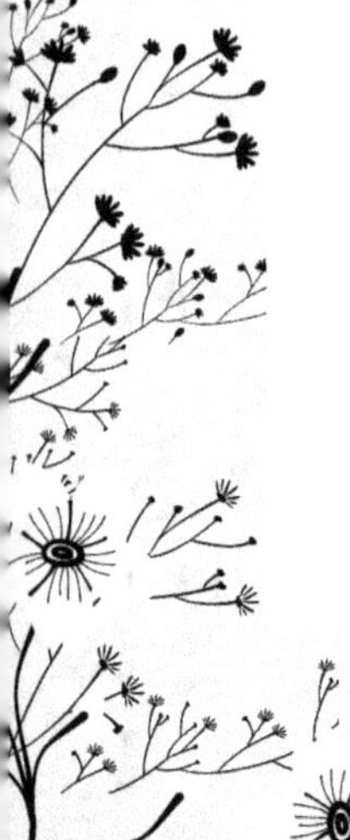

TODAY MY DAY WAS...

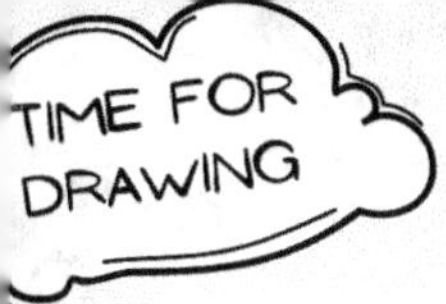

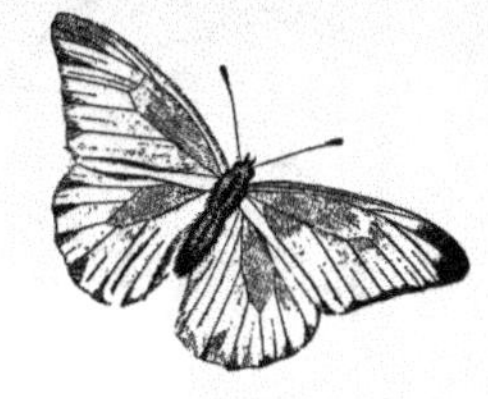

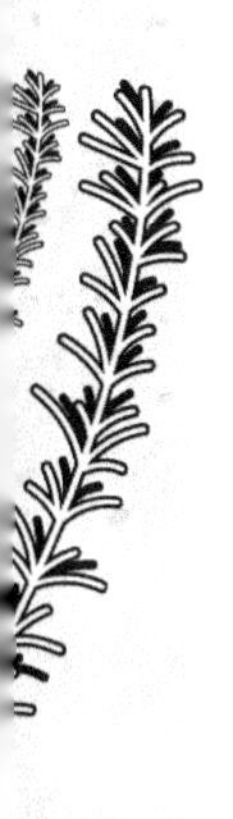

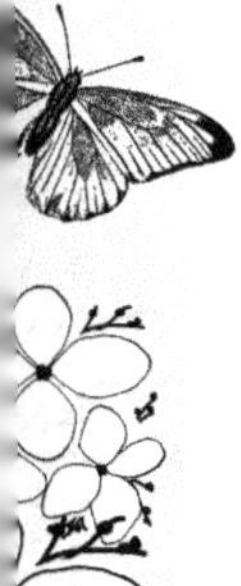

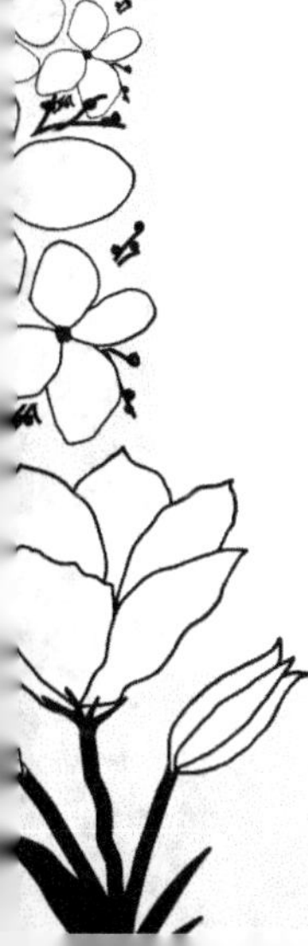

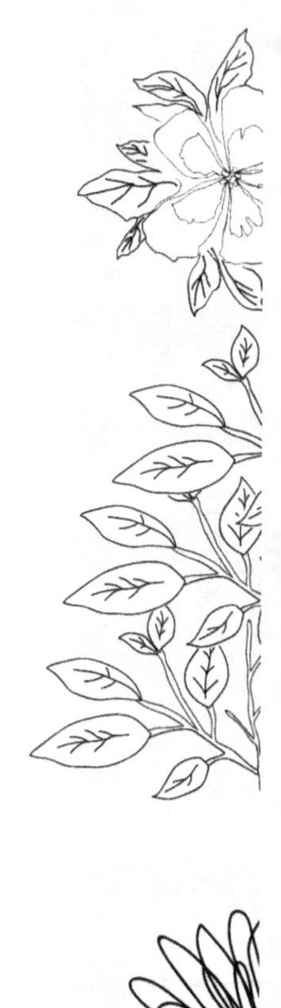

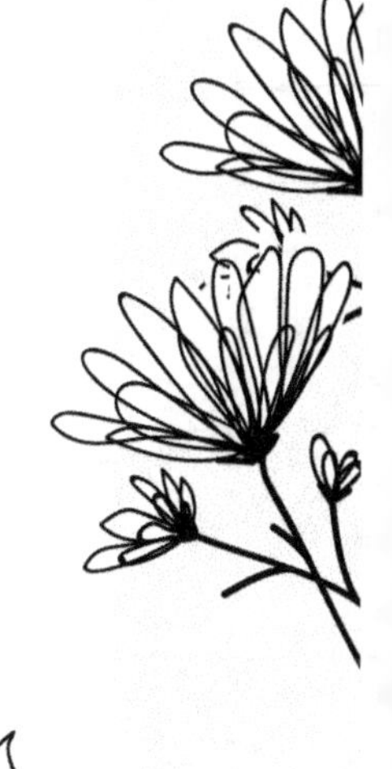

GOOD THINGS HAPPEN
TO ME ALL OF THE TIME!

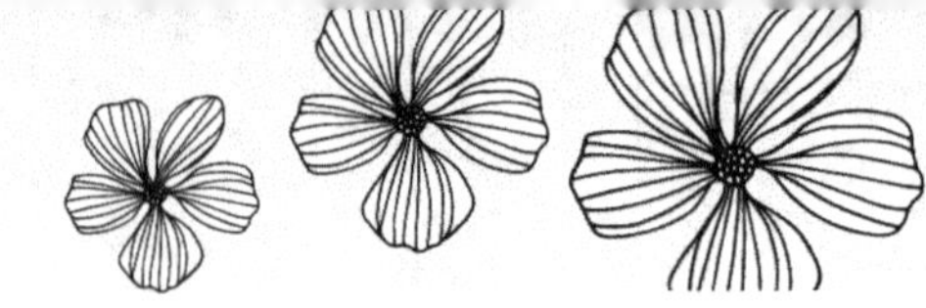

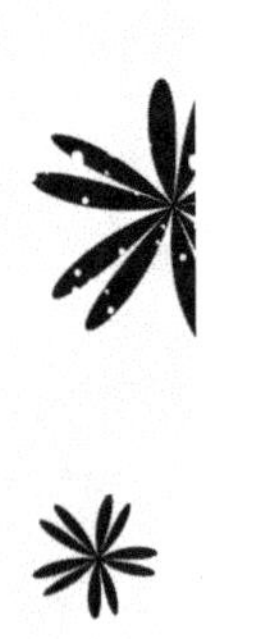

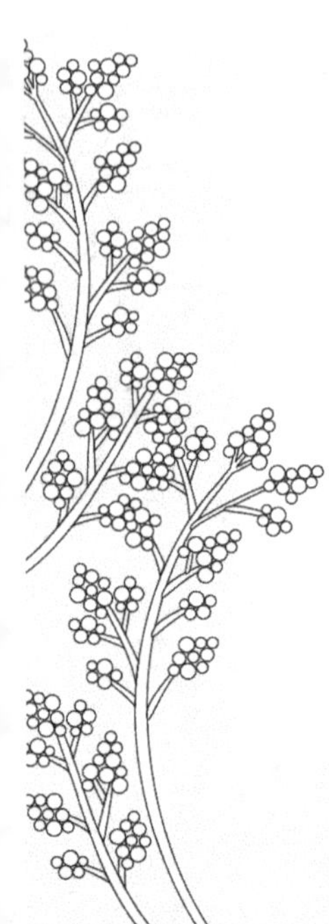

SOAR

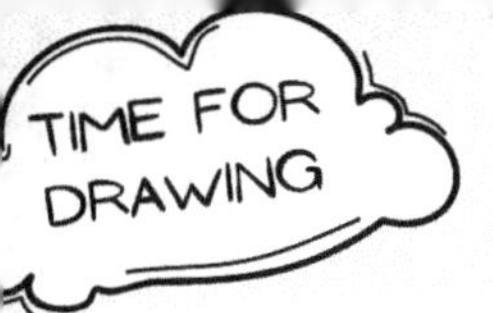

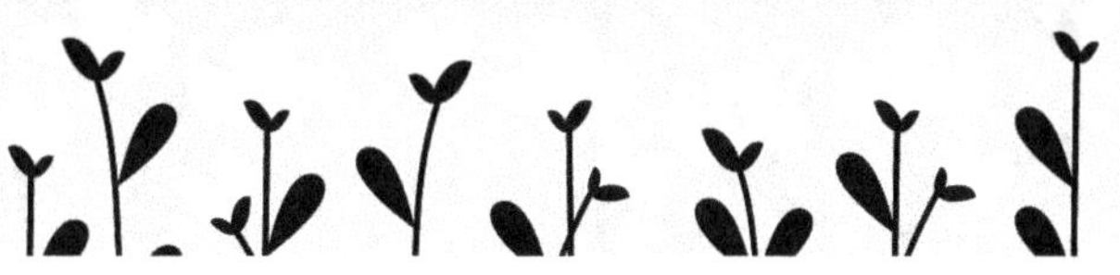
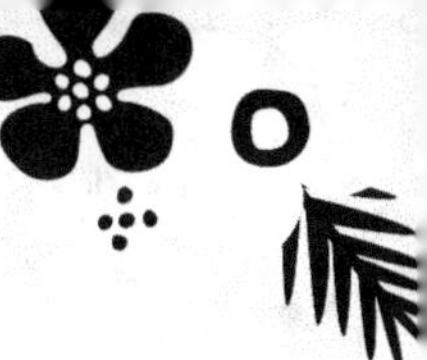

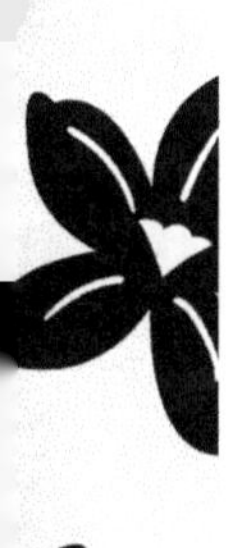
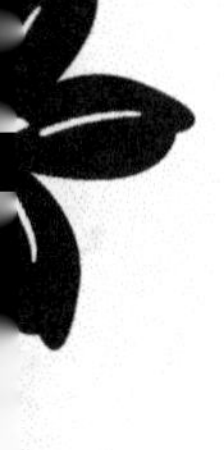
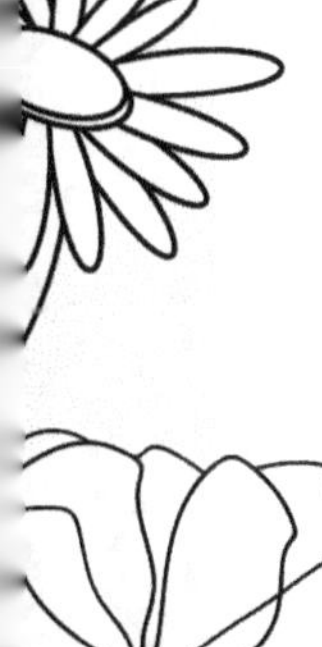
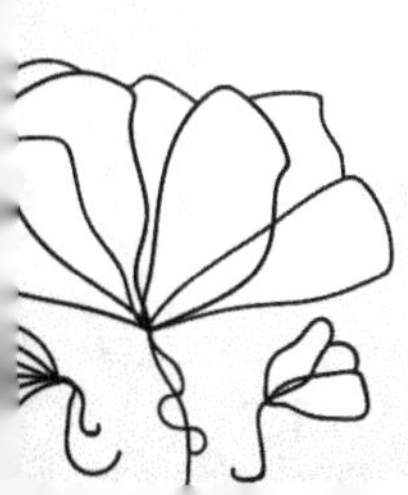
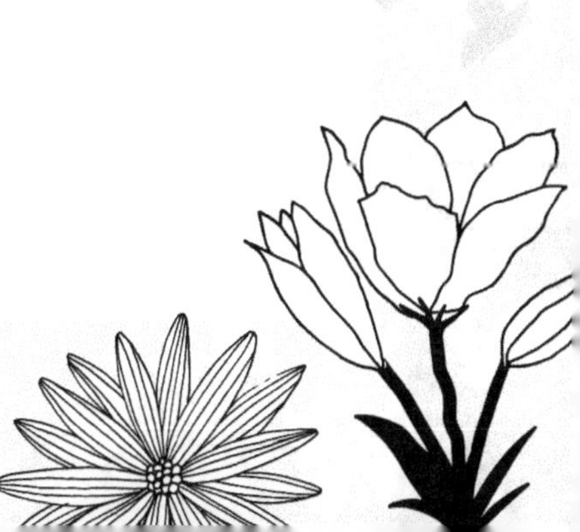

I LOVE MYSELF AND
OTHERS DO TOO!

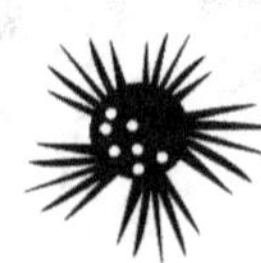

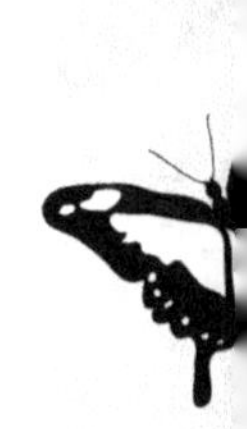

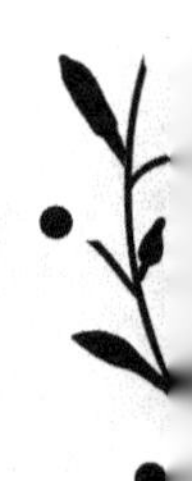

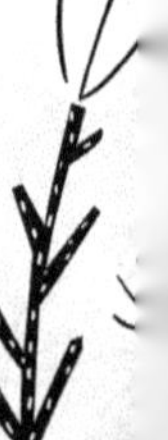

MY SUPER POWER IS ME!

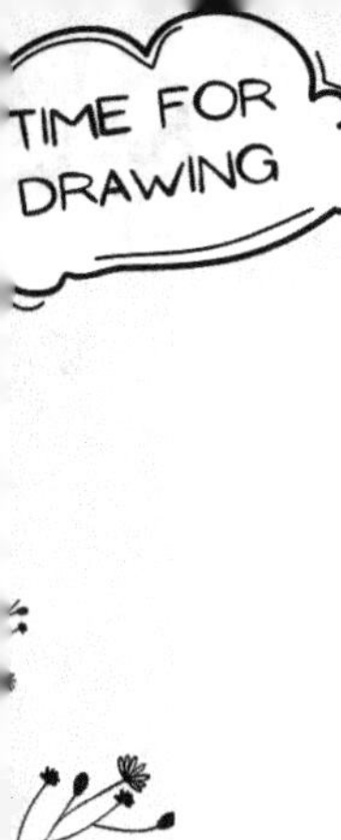
TIME FOR
DRAWING

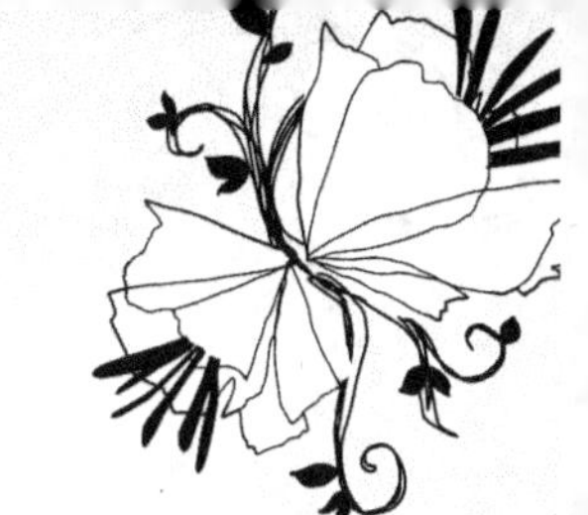

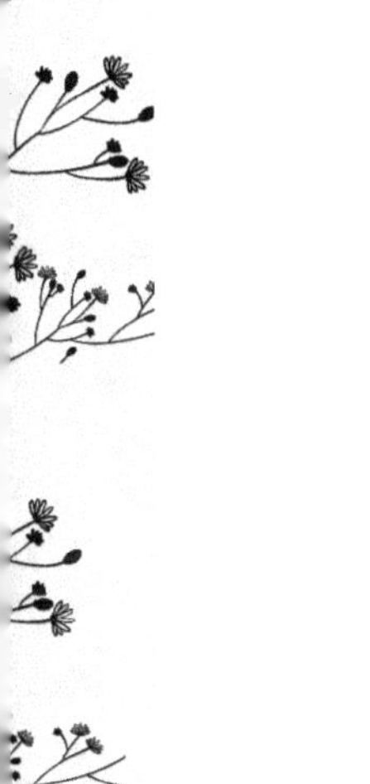

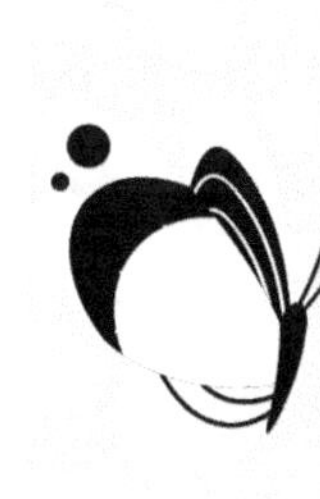

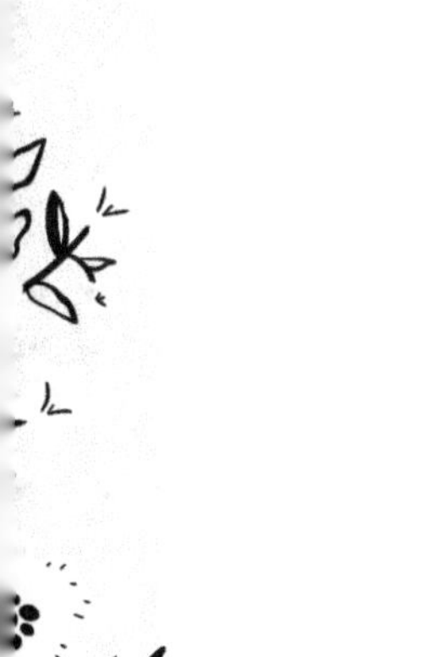

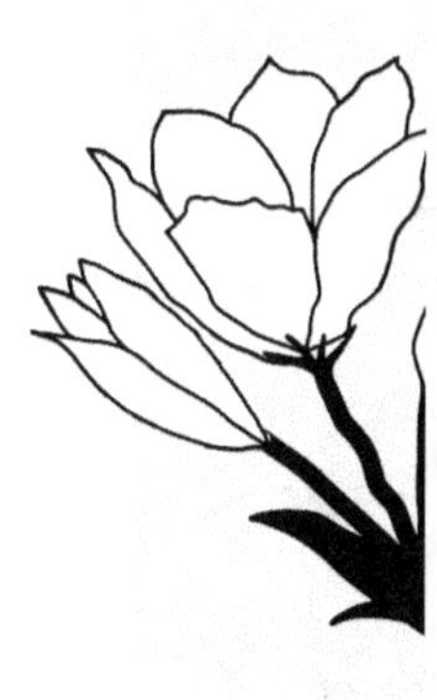

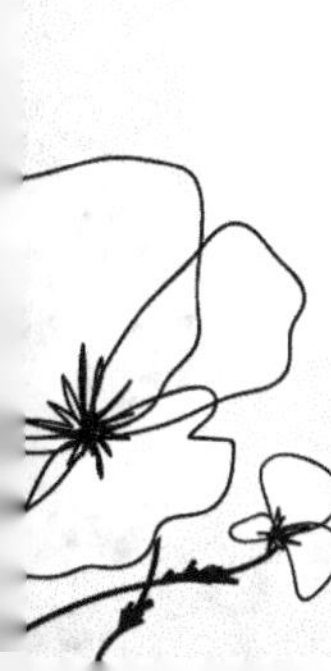

DREAM

enjoy!
enjoy!
enjoy!

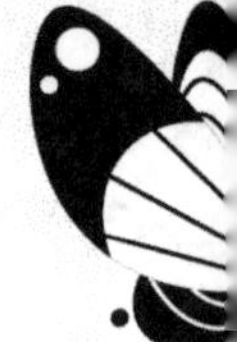

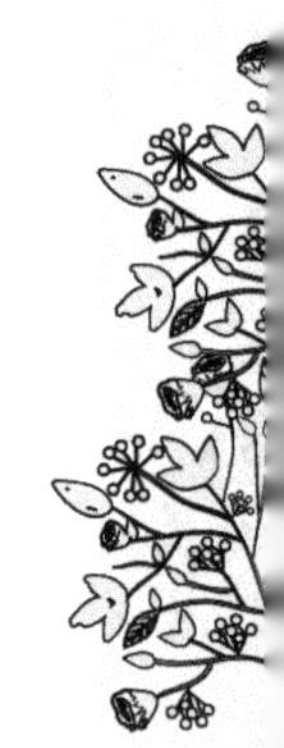

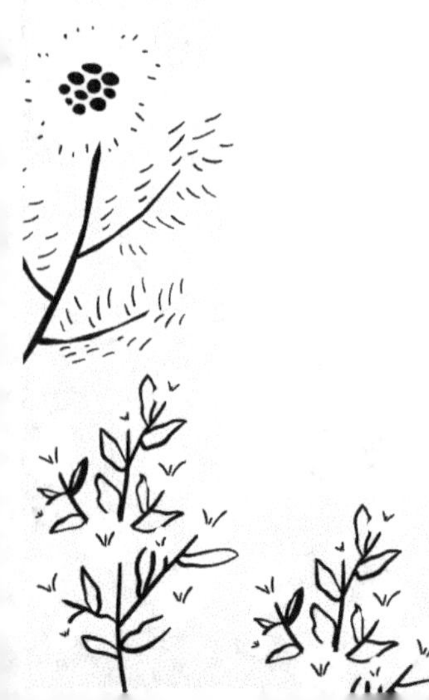

I AM MY HERO!

WHAT'S UP?

TIME FOR DRAWING
SOMETIMES CHANGE
CAN BE GOOD

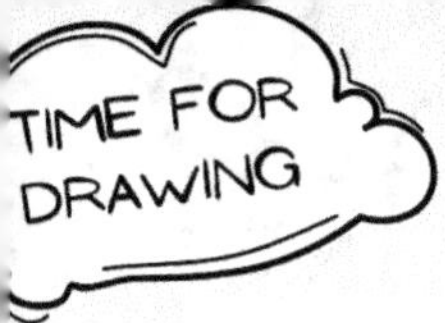

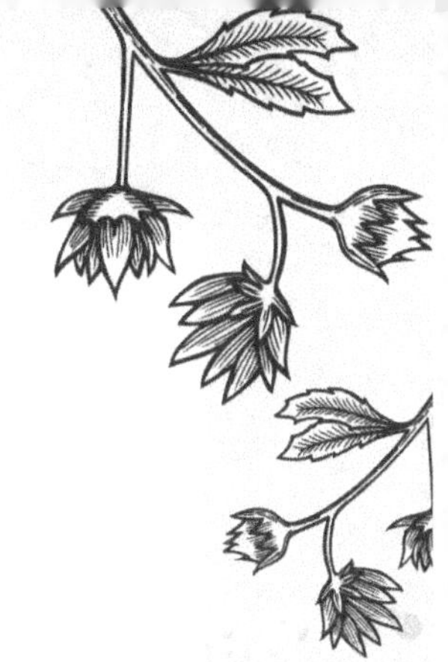

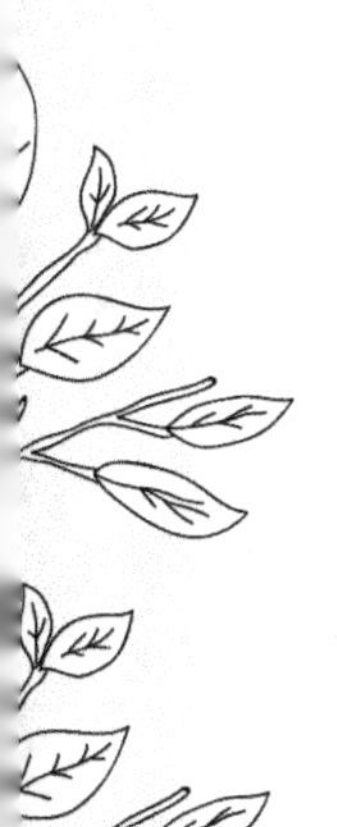

BREATHE

TIME FOR
DRAWING

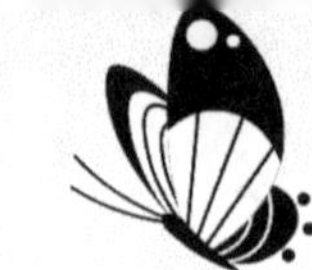

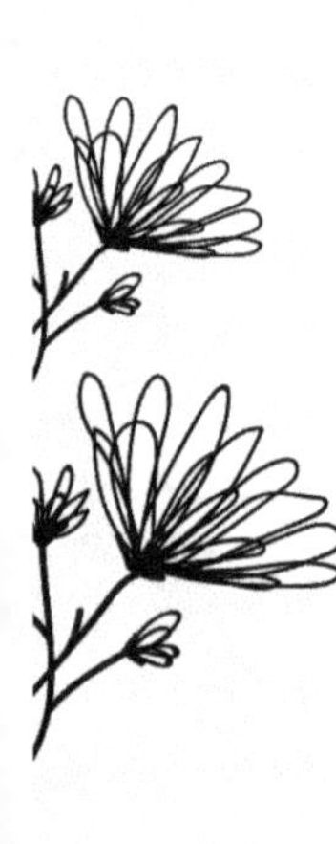

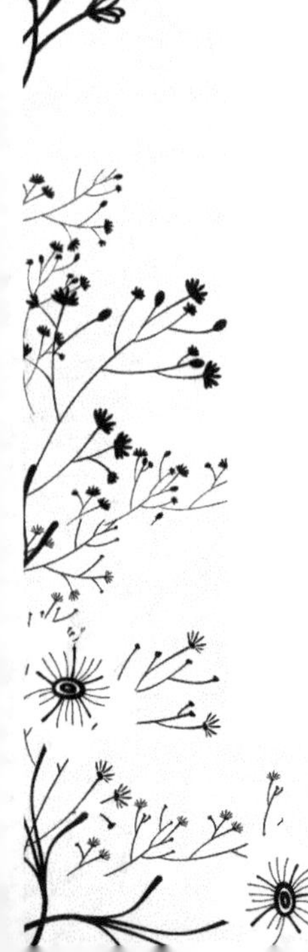
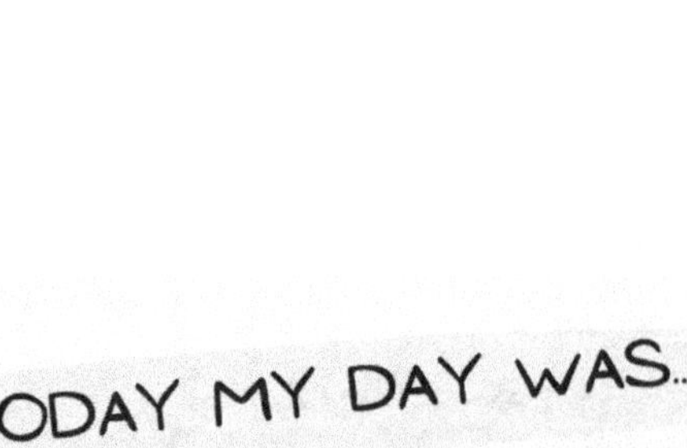
TODAY MY DAY WAS...

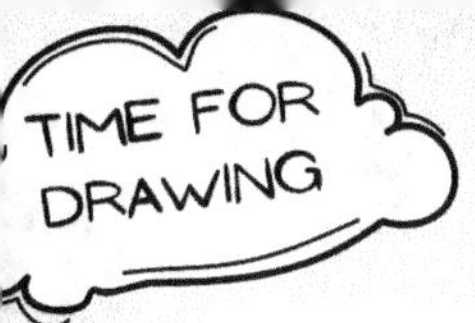

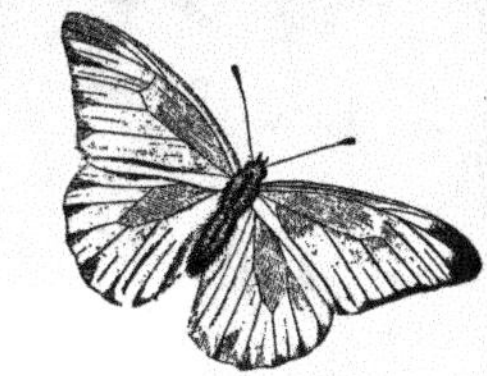

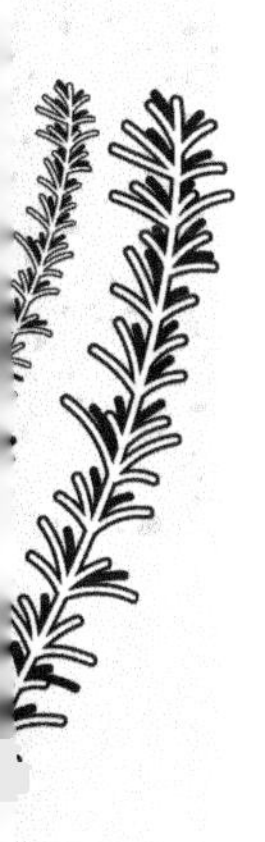

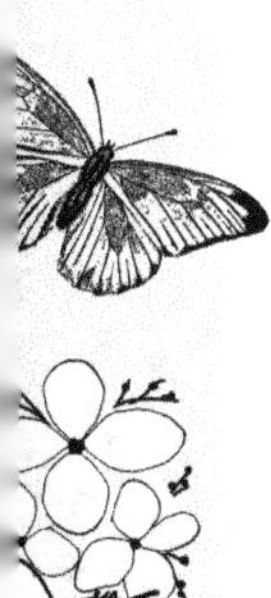

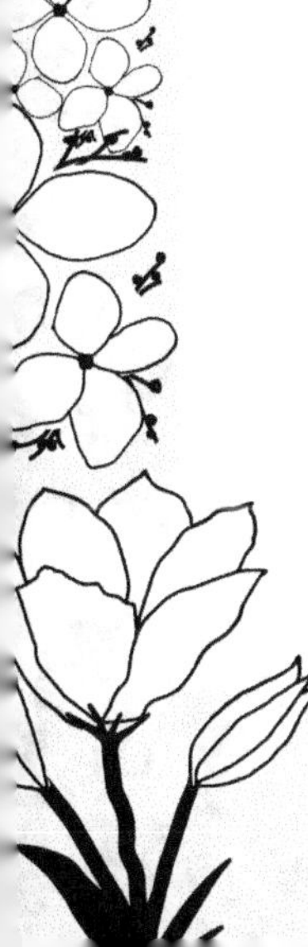

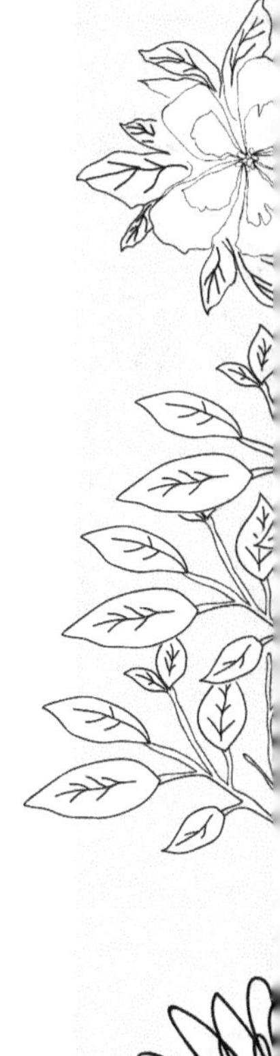

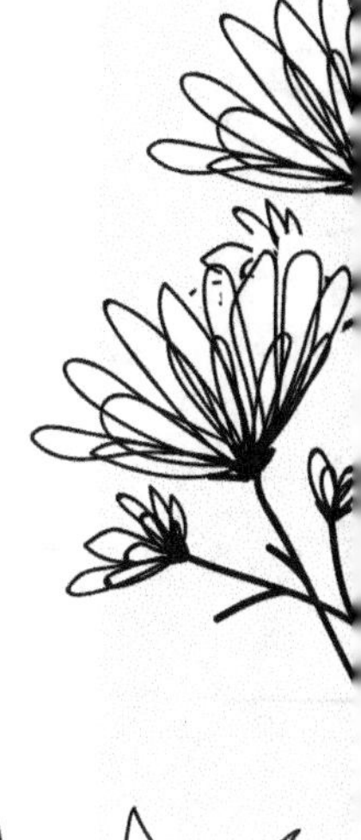

GOOD THINGS HAPPEN
TO ME ALL OF THE TIME!

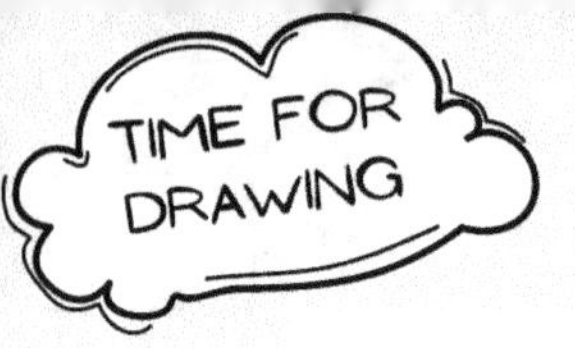

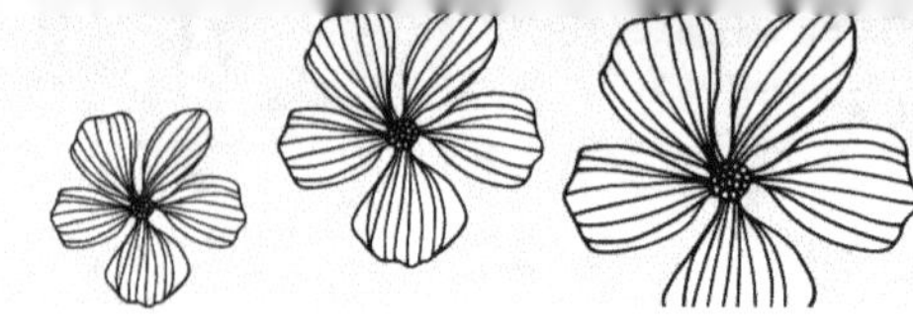

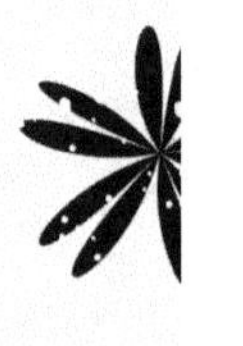

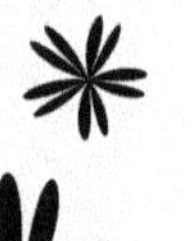

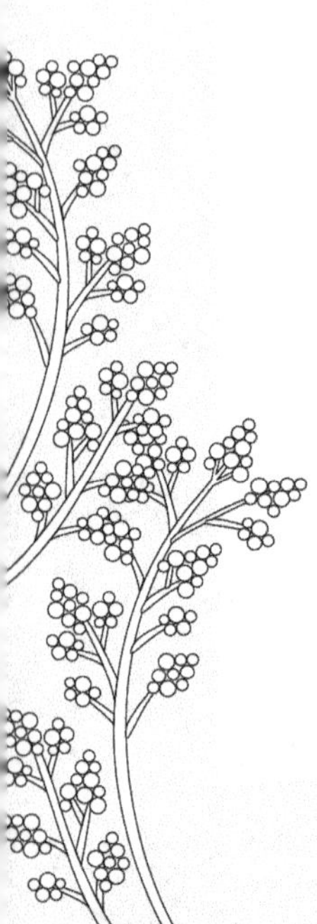

SOAR

TIME FOR DRAWING

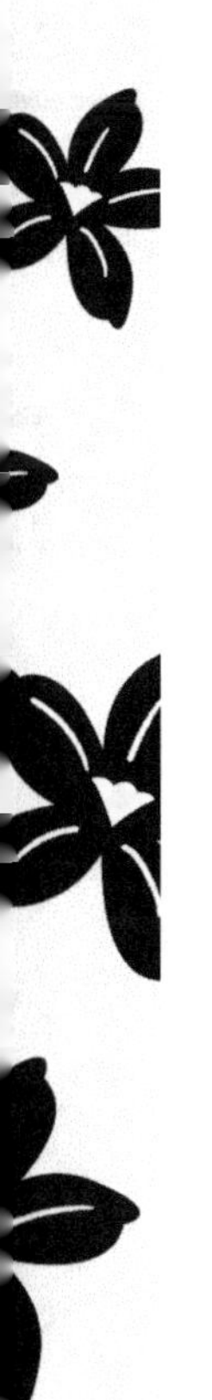

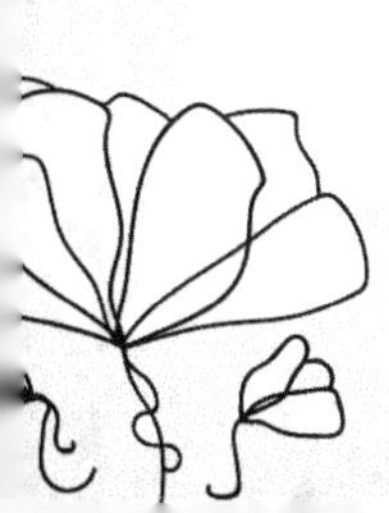

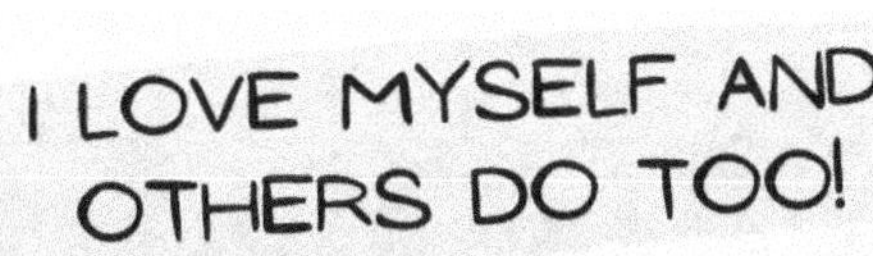
I LOVE MYSELF AND OTHERS DO TOO!

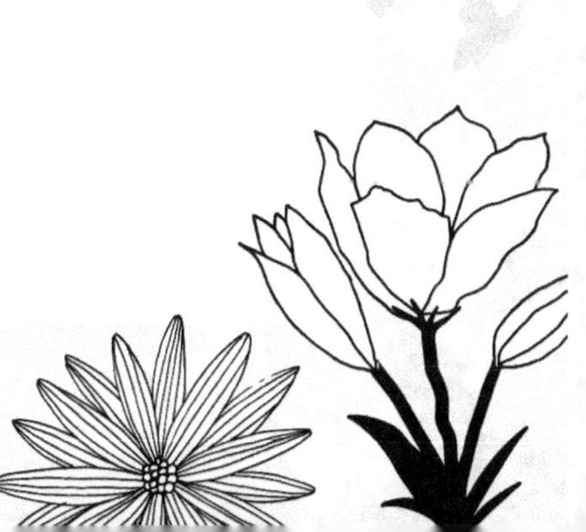

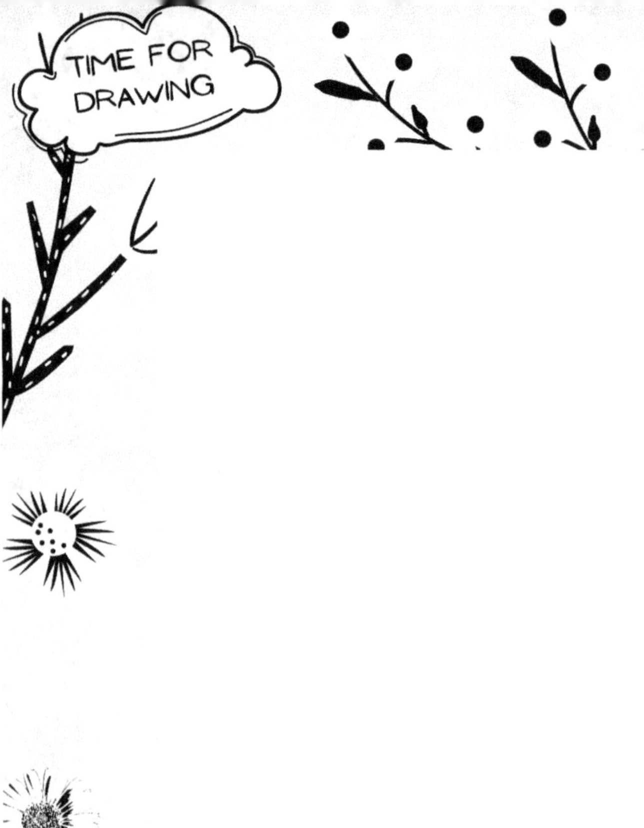

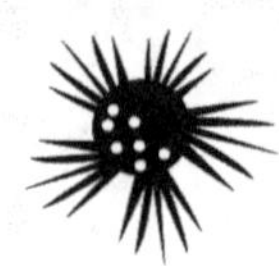

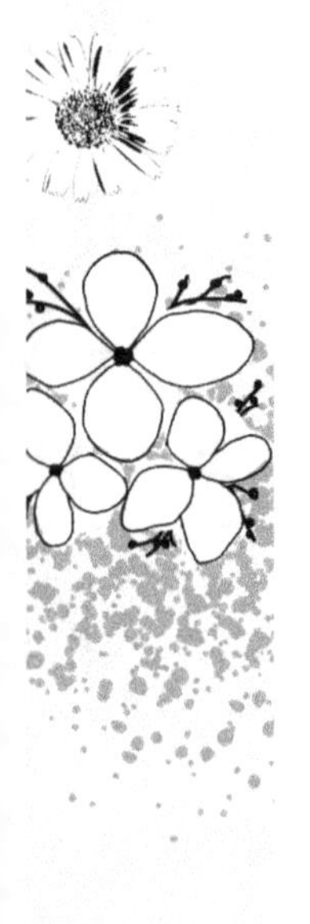
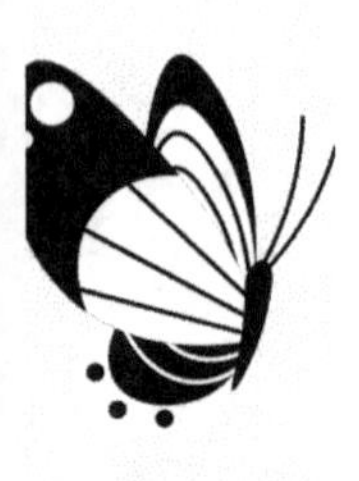
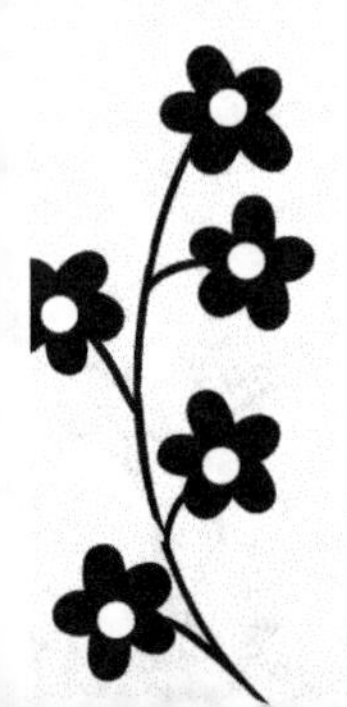
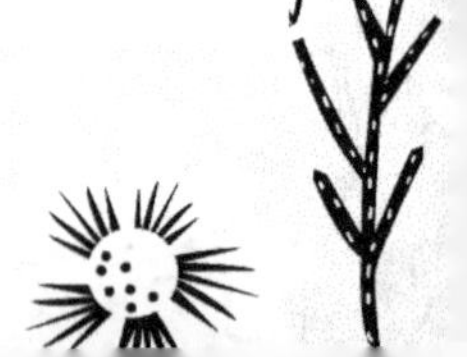

MY SUPER POWER IS ME!

TIME FOR
DRAWING

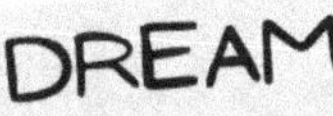

DREAM

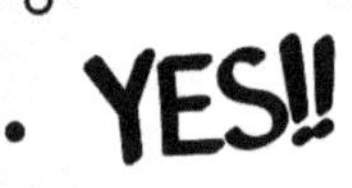

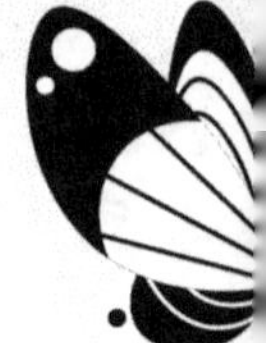

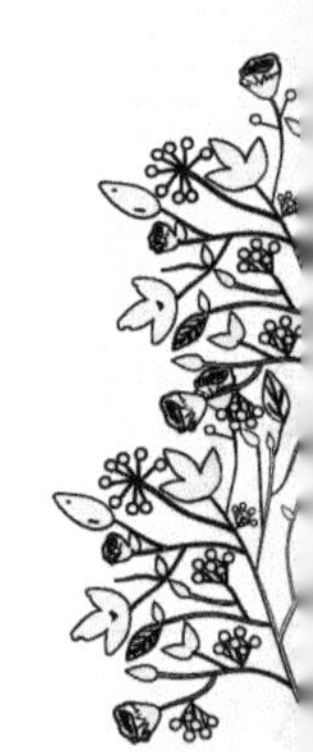

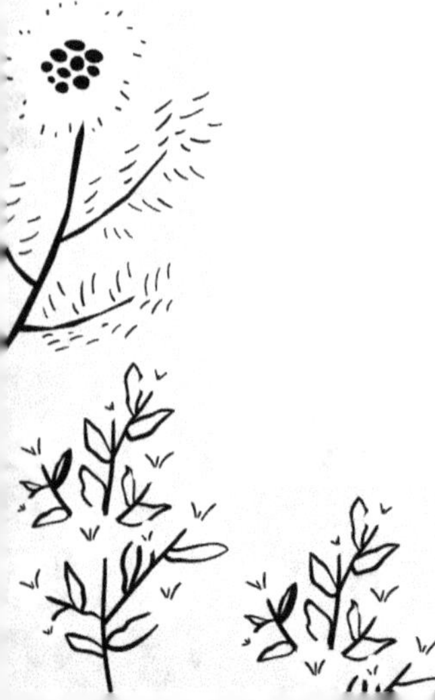

I AM MY HERO!

WHAT'S UP?

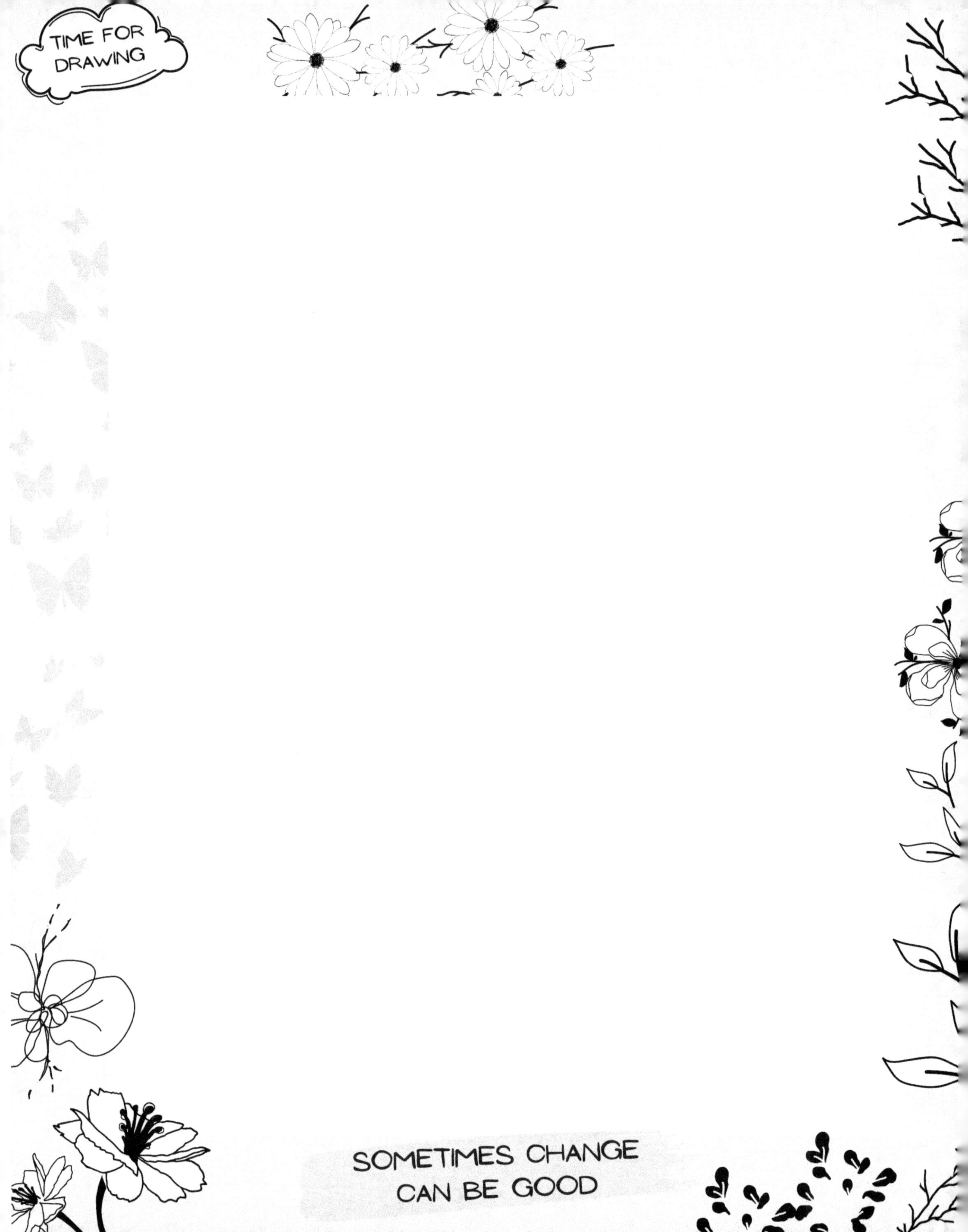

TIME FOR DRAWING
SOMETIMES CHANGE CAN BE GOOD

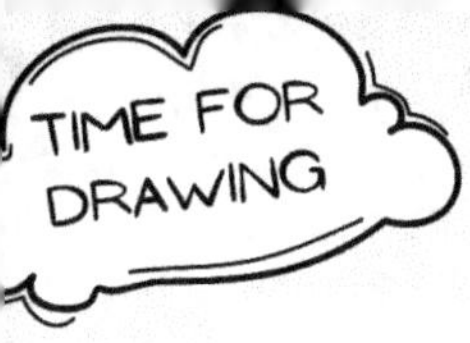

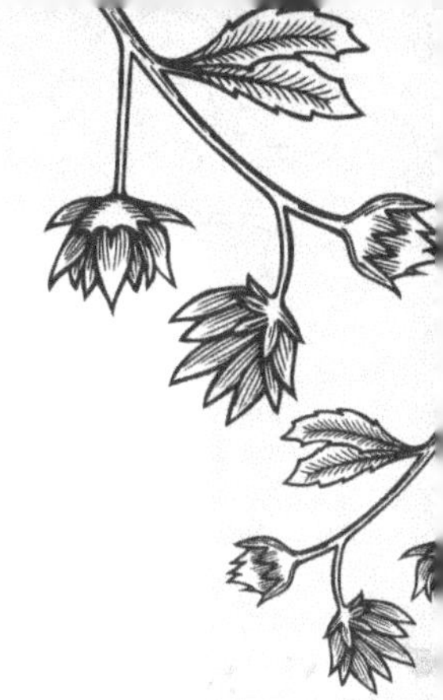

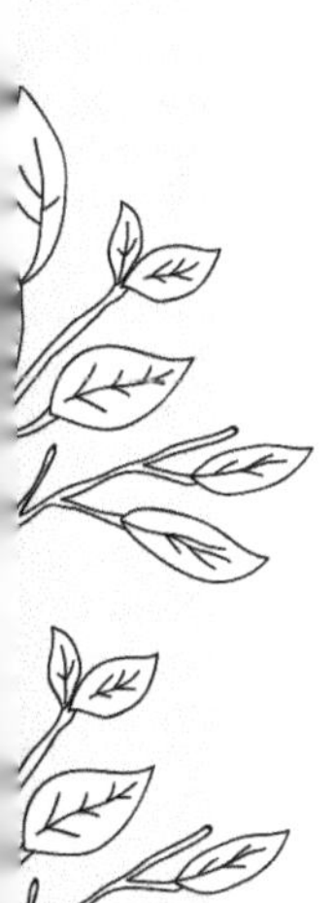

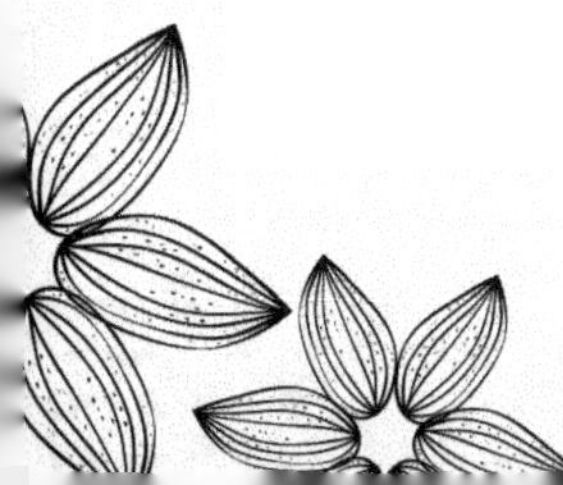

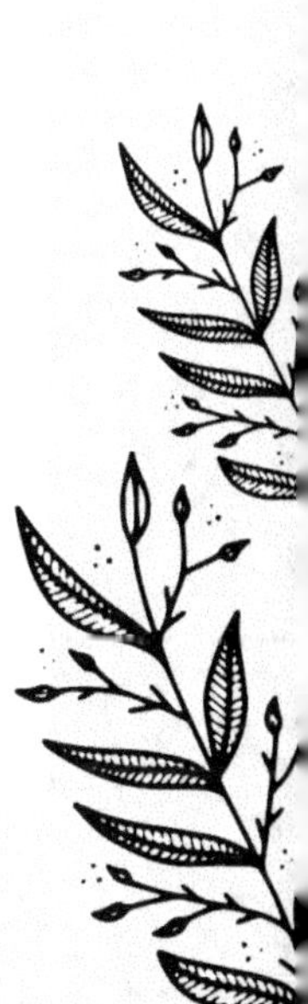

BREATHE

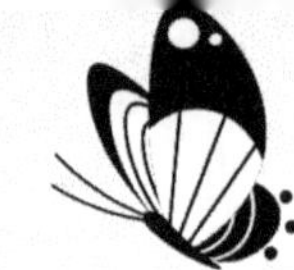
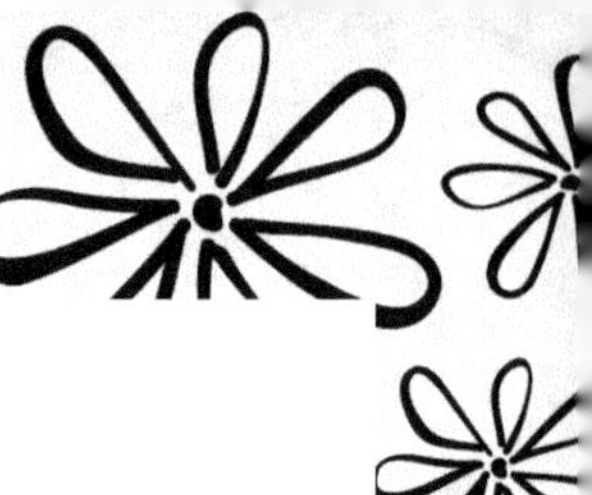

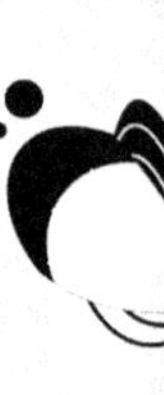
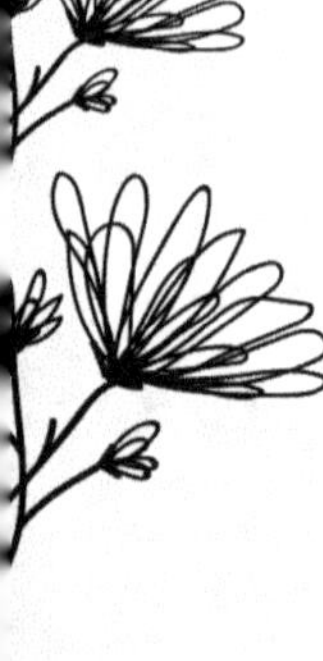
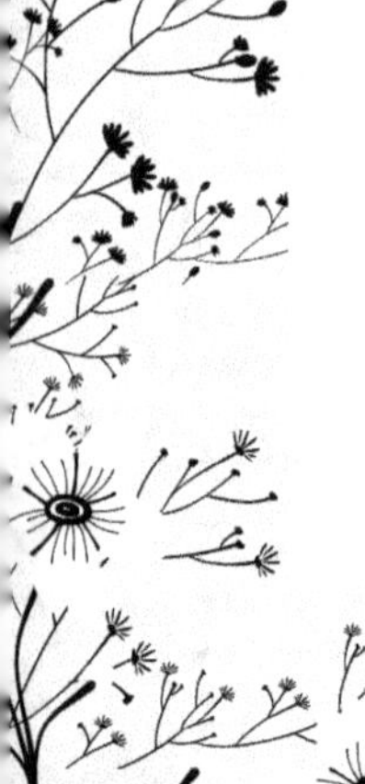

TODAY MY DAY WAS...

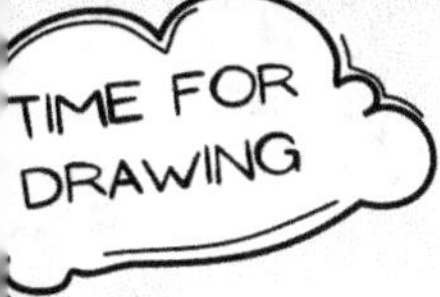

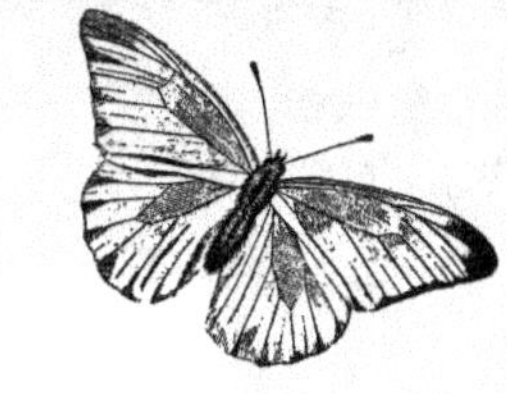

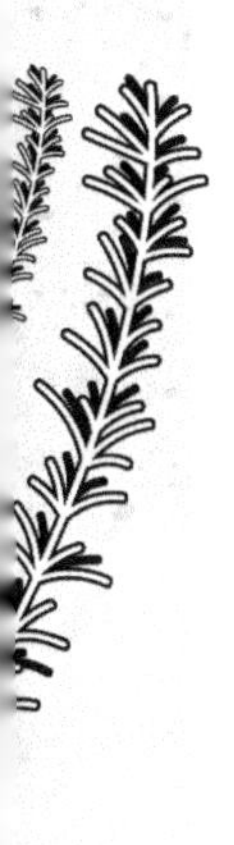

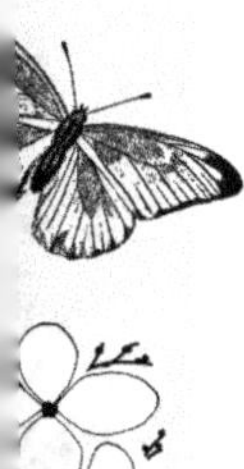

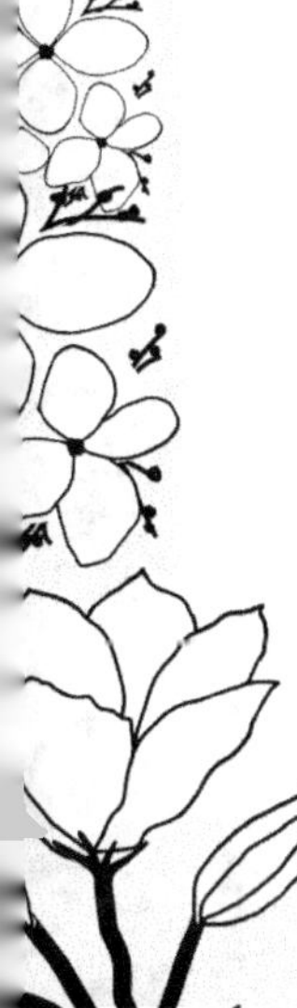

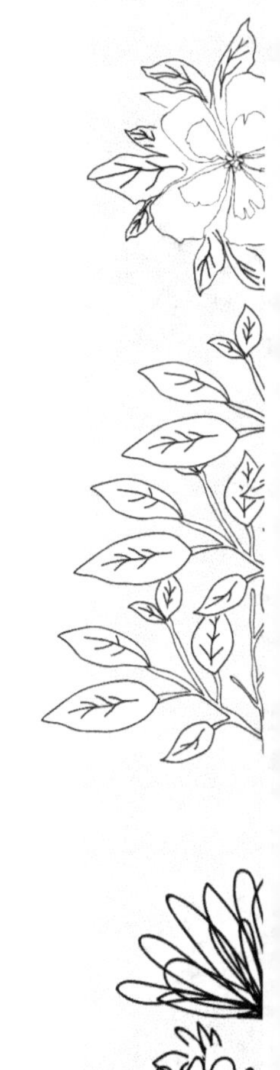

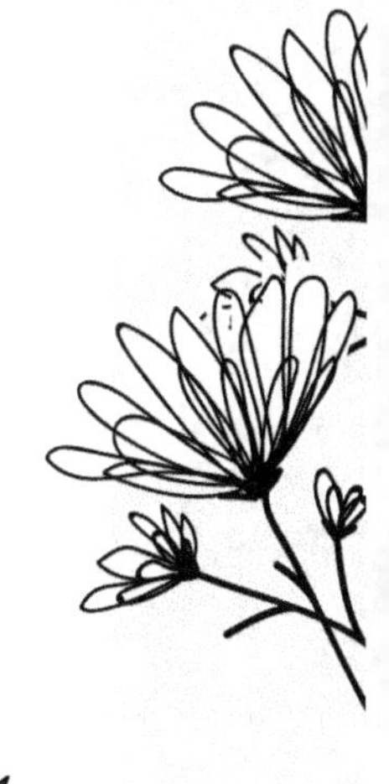

GOOD THINGS HAPPEN
TO ME ALL OF THE TIME!

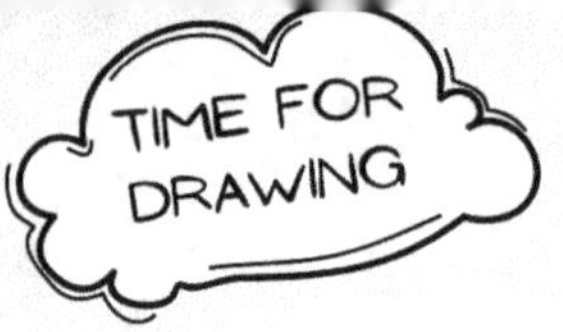

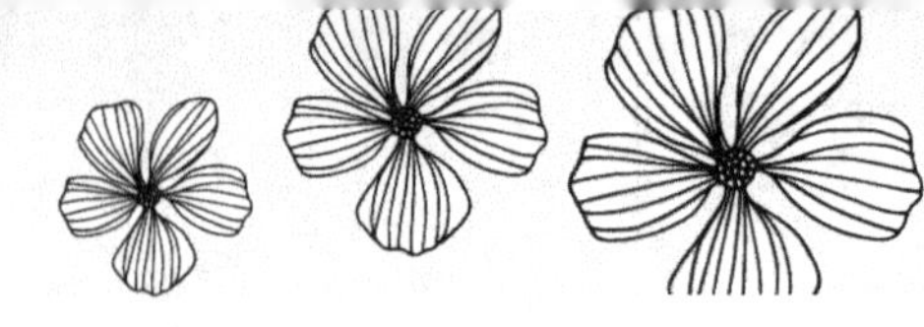

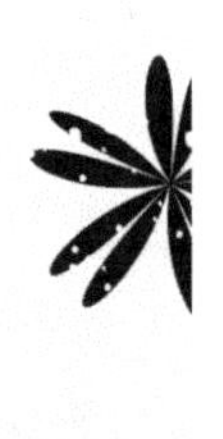

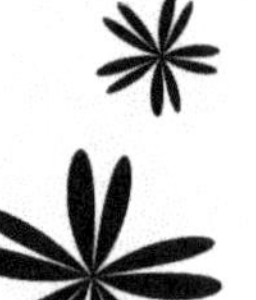

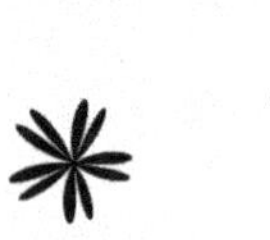

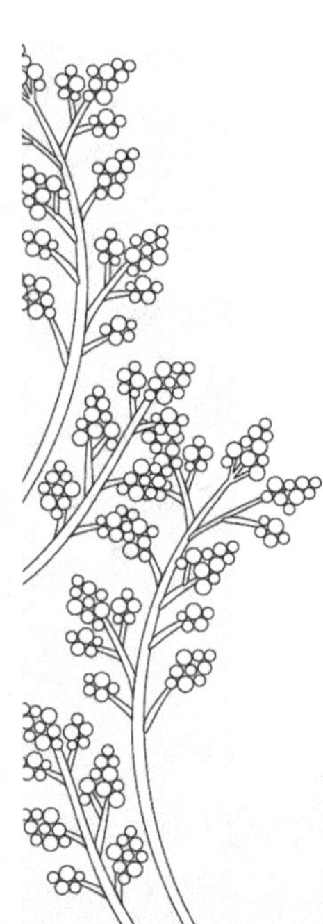

SOAR

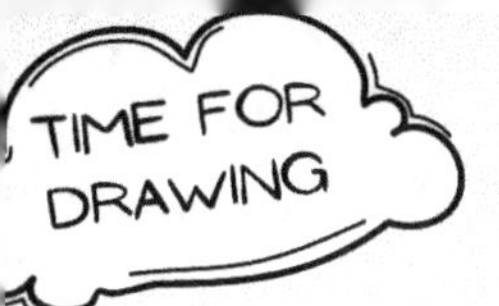
TIME FOR DRAWING

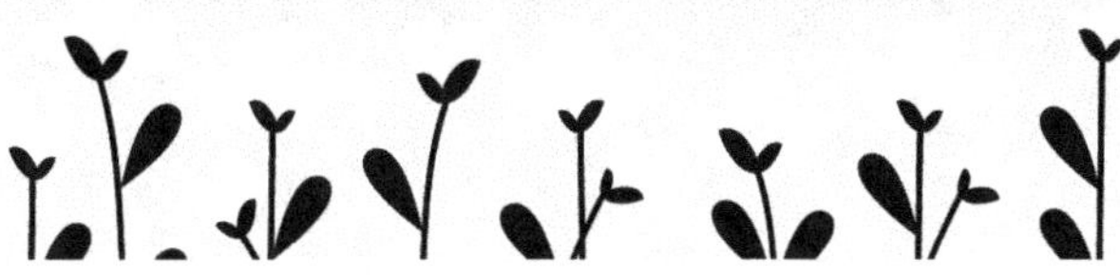

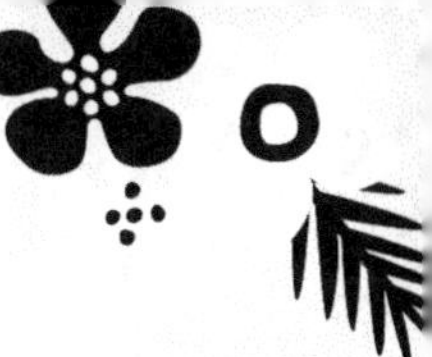

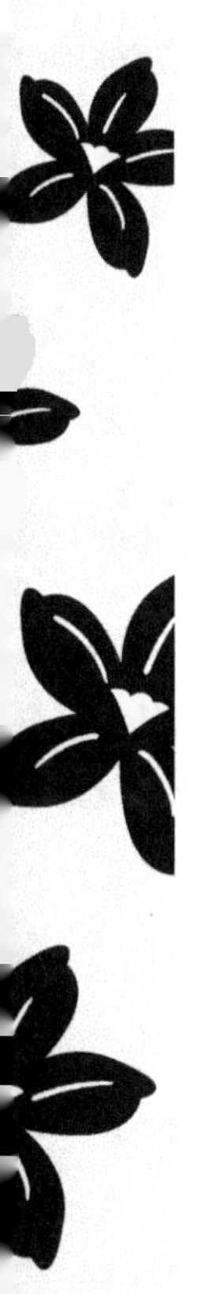

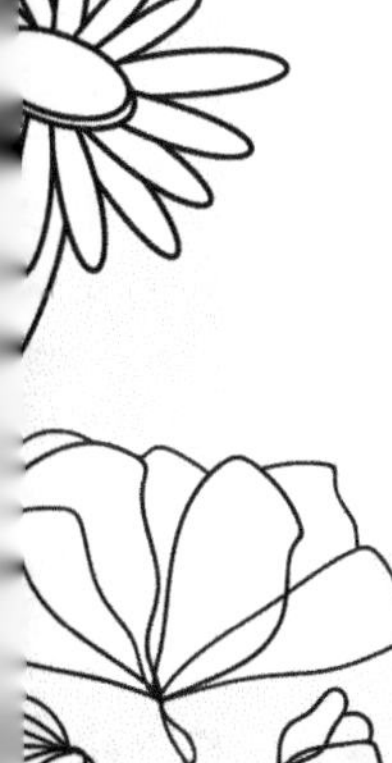

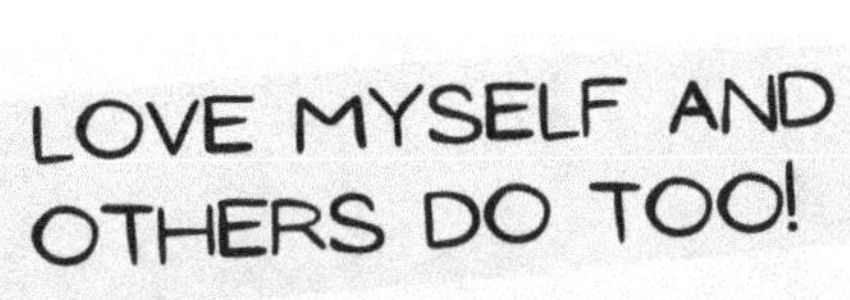
I LOVE MYSELF AND OTHERS DO TOO!

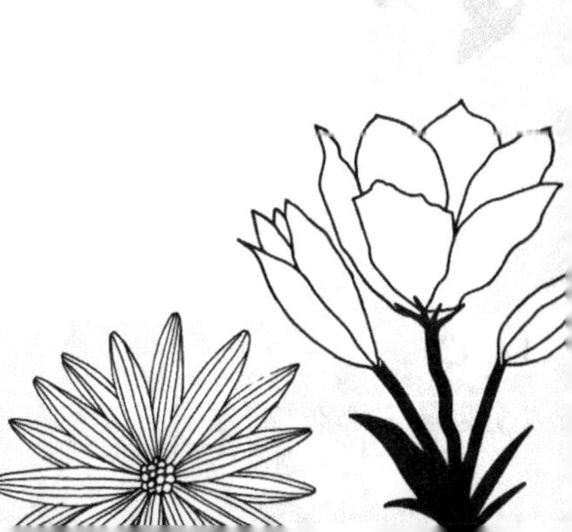